VEHICLE ENGINES

fuel consumption and air pollution

Edited by

M.S. Janota

Published by

Peter Peregrinus Ltd.

Southgate House, Stevenage,

Herts. SG1 1HQ, England

Ⓒ : 1974 Peter Peregrinus Ltd.
Reprinted 1978

ISBN : 0 901223 61 1

Library of Congress catalogue card number 74-83030

Printed in the United Kingdom by Unwin Brothers Limited, Old Woking, Surrey, England

Foreword

The importance of the problem of fuel consumption and air pollution is recognised
by everyone; therefore the conference convened by the Mechanical Engineering
Department of Queen Mary College, London, and attended by mechanical engineers,
was very much welcomed. I am quite sure that, so far as fuel consumption is concerned,
the car owner would welcome any increase in efficiency of the engine to cut down fuel
bills. Equally, the reduction of noise, particularly with heavy vehicle engines, is highly
to be desired. But maybe the item that attracts most attention at present is pollution
by the gases emitted by internal-combustion engines.

So much is written in the Press now about these problems that it is all the more
important that a scientific gathering of this kind should, by the presentation of papers
and by discussion, seek the facts existing in different situations. There is so much
scaremongering going on in this field that the general public never has an opportunity
really to assess the truth of the situation. The methods for establishing the levels of
pollution emitted by internal-combustion engines are not easy to devise, but methods do
exist now that go some way to providing these basic data. There are all sorts of other
problems that arise too in this field. We learn, for example, that nitrogen oxides
particularly are dangerous, but they act simply by their function as a photosensitiser,
for the production of smog-like conditions; but many people do not realise that in the
atmosphere there is a measurable concentration of ozone, and ozone is an equally
toxic material which is neglected in all situations of this kind. Therefore it is essential
to get some reliable physiological facts about the effect of these emissions on the
human organism.

There is, quite properly, a section on electric vehicles propelled by means of rechargeable
batteries of one kind or another. This, of course, is another very obvious way of cutting
down pollution and of economising on fuel in the end. There is one very fundamental
fact that must be borne in mind, and that is that these systems depend on chemical
reactions, and the fact of the matter is that the amount of chemistry one has got to
bring about to produce a significant amount of electrical power is very large indeed.
In other words, the batteries needed to produce a reasonable performance are large
compared with the size and weight of the vehicle itself, and there is not really very
much prospect of reducing their size and weight in the near future; but there are, of
course, specific fields in which this type of system has great attractions.

There is, however, an overriding matter. All these desired improvements involve
greater expenditure in transport. The question is the extent to which the user is
willing to pay.

Sir Harry Melville

Preface

Automotive power plant was identified, some years ago, as the cause of the persistent photochemical-smog problem around Los Angeles, and later around Tokyo and other major cities. In 1965, the Motor Vehicle Air Pollution Control Act in the US pinpointed the motor vehicle as a major source of air pollution. The rapid increase in the use of the motor car, particularly in areas of high population density, made people more conscious of the pollution danger. Inspired by public opinion, legislators, particularly in the US put tremendous pressure on car manufacturers, forcing them to cut drastically pollutant emission. The automotive industry resorted to all sorts of add-on devices and adaptations of the spark-ignition engine e.g. afterburners, catalysts, exhaust-gas recirculation, fuel injection, stratified charge systems, in order to achieve a saleable car. The result has been a considerable reduction in pollutant emission (nearly 90%), but not yet so as to meet all the requirements of the law applicable in 1976 for 100% durability. However, the consequences are an increased cost of the motor car, reduced engine performance and driveability, increased fuel consumption and a higher quality of maintenance required to keep the system effective. All the cost increases and inconvenience have to be borne by the motor vehicle user.

In recent years, the danger of our running out of world liquid-fuel resources has become a very important issue, under the name of 'Energy crisis' and savings in liquid fuel consumption have been advocated to preserve existing fuel resources. Research and development programmes designed to reduce pollutant emission found themselves on a collision course with the demands of the conservationist to reduce fuel consumption. For the car manufacturer and the power-plant designer, the demands generated enormous controversy. The confusion over further development of existing automotive power plant with increasing costs, or a replacement by an alternative system with better future potential, has become a very important question requiring very careful consideration. A conference was held at Queen Mary College, London, in April 1973, to discuss present day trends and discover possible future lines in the development of automotive power plant.

This book, which comprises a series of chapters by experts in the field, discusses possible developments and suitable future modifications of the present day well known prime movers to meet the air-pollution and liquid-fuel economy requirements. The chapters are based on the lectures given during the conference. It is hoped that it will be of value to those interested in the problem by providing useful information in the fight to reduce air pollution and preserve fuel resources.

London   M.S. Janota

fuel consumption
air pollution
internal combustion engines

rotary engines
gas turbines
Stirling engines
steam engines
electric vehicles

Contents

Part 1
Statement of the problem

1 Road vehicles and the environment

Prof. M.W. Thring, Sc.D., C.Eng., F.I.Mech.E., F.I.E.E.,M.I.Chem.E., F.Inst.P., F.Inst F.,F.R.Ae.S.
Professor of Mechanical Engineering, Queen Mary College, London, England

1 Statement of the long-term problem of road transport

Anyone who has young children or grandchildren must be concerned about what kind of world they will live in, in the 21st century. As soon as one tries to peer into the future, one sees a number of disconcerting facts, among which the following are particularly relevant to our present purpose:

(a) The gap in the standard of living between ordinary people in the rich, developed countries on the one hand, and poor people in the rich countries and the vastly greater number of poor people in the undeveloped countries (about two-thirds of the total world population of $3 \cdot 7 \times 10^9$) on the other hand, has increased since the Second World War, and is still increasing at the present time. This is partly due to the rate of increase of the population of the poor countries, but also largely due to the fact that the rich countries have made no serious attempt to help the others industrialise themselves. At a recent Stockholm conference on the environment, the main message from the underdeveloped countries was: 'we want to be able to pollute as much as the rich countries do'. It is quite clear that, as long as we judge our success by our accumulation of status symbols, so with the Africans, South Americans, Asians and other inhabitants of undeveloped countries want similar status symbols as soon as they learn of their existence. In particular, one can say that every family in the world will want the benefits of a car by the year 2000, and, if they do not get it, the resulting world tensions will lead at least to a multiplication of the present local conflicts, terrorism and violence, and, at worst, to global war.

It is also certain that the population of the world will increase to at least 7000 million by the early part of the 21st century unless a world war breaks out. However, if everyone in the world gets a really good education and can earn a really good standard of living by the 21st century, there is a hope that the world population can be voluntarily levelled off at about that figure.

One conclusion from this first consideration (the one essential condition that our descendants in the 21st century live a decent life) is that everyone of the 7000 million people will have to have perfectly adequate means of transport. If we define adequate means of transport for the present purposes as a family car, supplemented by safe, comfortable and convenient air, rail, ship, underground and bus public transport, we have to work out how we could run 1400 000 000 cars in the small land area of this globe.

(b) The most extreme society from the point of view of the lavish use of fuel is the USA which, with 6% of the world's population, uses 35% of the annual fuel and energy of the whole world. Every US citizen — man, woman or child — is responsible for the consumption of two tons of gasoline in cars every year. If all the 7×10^9 people in the 21st century used as much as the present-day US citizen does, the world would require 14 000 million tons of gasoline a year, while the Rymans 1967 estimate (Reference 1) of the total world reserves of petroleum was 260 000 million tons. Thus cars alone would use all the world resources in less than 20 years.

This leads inevitably to the conclusion that the responsible world citizen of the future will not expect to use more than about one-tenth of the present US consumption of energy in his cars and other transport vehicles.

(c) It is becoming a commonplace observation that life for ordinary people in rich countries is deteriorating in quality as society gets more affluent. There are a number of reasons for this deterioration, which is evidenced by the increase in (i) people opting out of ordinary life (suicides, drugs, alcoholism, separated communities, dropouts); (ii) stress illnesses and nervous breakdowns; (iii) violence against individuals associated with fear, hatred and mistrust. Among the ways in which the car as an affluent-society status symbol particularly damages the quality of life are:

(1) air pollution by car exhausts
(2) traffic jams
(3) accidents
(4) vehicle noise and vibration
(5) unconscious guilt feelings that people are starving and suffering from lack of common necessities while the mechanical status symbol is treated with loving care
(6) motorways destroying the countryside.

It is greatly to be hoped that enough people will decide to replace the affluent society with its worship of status symbols with a society that regards the quality of life as infinitely more important than the possession of objects beyond those necessary to enable the individual to realise all his or her creative possibilities. However, it is clear that the gift, to an ordinary family of freedom to travel from door to door in family privacy with any luggage or domestic animals, that a car provides, is, in itself, a very real increase in freedom, provided that it is not associated with the above mentioned six contributions of the car to the lowering of the quality of human life.

Here we are particularly concerned with the engine that propels the vehicle, and the engine is the consumer of fuel and the principal maker of noise and air pollution; so we have to consider how engines can be developed that consume even less fuel per passenger mile than the 40 mile/gal European passenger cars when carrying four people, and that reduce air pollution and noise to acceptable minimum values.

2   The fuel resources available

In 'The energy resources of the earth' [Energy and Power Scientific American Book] (W.H. Freeman & Co., 1971), p. 35, M. King Hubbert gives a chart for the estimated petroleum reserves of the continents. These are (all in 10^9 barrels, about 8 barrels = 1 ton)

Western hemisphere:	Canada	96
	USA	200
	Latin America	225
	Europe	20
	Africa	250
	Middle East	600
	Far East	200
	USSR and China	500

These are based on Rymans estimates (Standard Oil Company of New Jersey), and are for ultimate crude-oil production including off-shore areas, oil already produced, proved and probable reserves, and future discoveries. The very small reserves in Europe compared with our high consumption is one fact to be considered; the other urgent fact is the approaching exhaustion of US oil reserves: this is already causing concern, so that some central heating and jet flights had to be stopped last winter, and, if the US demand continues to rise at the present rate of 1% per year, the USA might have to import as much from the Middle East by 1980 as the entire Middle East produced in 1970. The estimates of the Alaskan oil are 30-50 x 10^9 bbl, but the USA uses over 3 x 10^9 bbl per year at the present, so that the supply to the USA could last only some ten years.

The complete table of the world's recoverable fossil fuels is given by King Hubbert as follows:

Coal and lignite	7·6 x 10^{12} tons	=	55·9 x 10^{15} thermal kWh	89%
Natural gas	10^{16} ft^3	=	2·94 "	4·7%
Liquid petroleum	2000 x 10^9 bbl	=	3·25 "	5·2%
Tar sand oil	300 x 10^9 bbl	=	0·51 "	0·8%
Shale oil	190 x 10^9 bbl	=	0·32 "	0·5%

The tar sand oil has to be recovered by scraping up the sand, treating it with steam and then cracking the tar to leave half the calorific value as petro coke whereas the shale must be mined and then heated in a retort to drive off the oil; so both these processes are last resorts, likely to be used when all the easily pumped oil and natural gas have been used. Coal can be converted into liquid fuel by hydrogenation and Fischer Tropsch synthesis, but both processes require 5-6 tons of coal to make a ton of oil. Coal can also be burnt in a power station to make electricity that is used to electrolyse water to give pure hydrogen as a feasible vehicle fuel.

For many years, it has been the official policy of the rich countries that we do not need to worry about oil exhaustion by our fuel-greedy cars, because we shall have developed nuclear-fission reactors to produce electricity so cheaply that we can afford to electrolyse water and use compressed hydrogen as our transport fuel. All the nuclear-fission power stations so far built are nonbreeder, and this means that the only fuel is the rare isotope U^{235}, which occurs to the extent of one part in 140 in natural uranium. When 1 g of U^{235} undergoes fission, it produces as much heat as the combustion of 2·7 tons of coal, or 24 MWh of electricity. Now the non-Communist world's resources of reasonably concentrated uranium (that can be mined at a price of less than $10 per lb) are estimated by R.L. Faulkner (Resources and man, p.223) to be 1·6 million tons, so that only 12 000 tons of easily obtainable U^{235} are available, and this is thermally equivalent to roughly 30 000 million tons of coal, or less than 1/100th of the estimated world's coal resources.

Unless, therefore, we develop breeder reactors to replace all new nonbreeder reactors in the next 10-15 years, we shall be making such inroads into the accessible rich uranium sources that this idea will become a pipedream. There are still a number of unsolved problems with breeder reactors, so that most new reactors being installed at the moment are of the nonbreeder type. On the other hand, breeder reactors mean we have 200-300 times as much fissile fuel, because, then, not only can we burn up all the

4

uranium (U^{235}) but also convert thorium into a fissile material. The controlled-fusion reactor remains an unsolved problem even in the laboratory; so one cannot count on it as a way out of our troubles.

Hydrogen is not a convenient fuel, as it has a relatively low calorific value per unit volume and a very low boiling point, so that it requires very heavy high-pressure steel bottles to carry it. Methane has about three times the calorific value per unit volume, and, although it has about eight times the density of hydrogen, this does not matter, because the bottle is much heavier than the fuel in both cases. Methane has the advantage over all other hydrocarbons that it is almost impossible to have soot in the products of incomplete combustion, and it is a very good fuel for spark-ignition car engines, apart from the bottle weight problem. Since natural gas is nearly pure methane, and natural gas exists in the Earth's crust to an extent comparable with the total liquid-petroleum resources, this is an obvious fuel supplement. In the Lacq area in the south of France, natural gas has, for 15 years, been supplied at power stations to lorries carrying a rack of bottles on the roof. In the Middle East, most of the natural gas is burnt uselessly at the well head.

Methyl alcohol is also a very good fuel for the spark-ignition engine, and it can be made from fermentation of agricultural products (its old name was 'wood alcohol') or from methane, and it can be carried in a light tank, like gasoline or petrol.

One must conclude that a responsible attitude to the needs of the whole of mankind in the 21st century requires that

(a) petroleum and natural gas be used to a much greater fraction on transport

(b) road vehicles be developed with far less fuel consumption per passenger mile.

3 How much fuel does road transport really need?

The fuel consumption of a car, in joules per passenger mile, depends primarily on the following factors:

(a) size of the engine

(b) weight of the vehicle

(c) number of passengers

(d) efficiency of the engine and transmission.

As far as (c) is concerned, there seems little doubt that humanity will be unable to afford the energy consumption involved in a single person travelling in a car built for four or six people, but this is not a technological problem; so there is no point in discussing it further here. The weight of the vehicle will have to be reduced considerably compared with most present vehicles designed to carry the same number of passengers, subject to the two other conditions that must certainly be satisfied if the private car is to survive into the 21st century, namely greatly improved safety for passengers and pedestrians and cars lasting a lifetime to conserve raw materials and fuel used in manufacture.

The size of the engine is largely conditioned at present by the status-symbol concept of rapid acceleration, a concept that will have to be completely buried in the not too distant future, as it is largely responsible, not only for high fuel consumption, but also for engines designed to emit unburnt or partially burnt fuel, and for a great part of the vehicle noise that makes the lives of people living near a city street or a motorway so intolerable. It also encourages the competitive driving that leads to so many accidents.

5

The high-acceleration advertising concept is almost as absurd as the 120 mile/h car in a country with a speed limit of 70 mile/h. There is no doubt therefore, that, if the private car survives in the 21st century, it will have the smallest and most economical engine that can be devised.

One of the greatest problems, both in minimising fuel consumption and in minimising air pollution and noise, is that due to the rapid changes in engine power and revolutions needed in traffic driving. The engine cannot give its best performance over such a wide range, but it is during the transients that it is impossible to relate air and fuel intake accurately to each cylinder. Petrol injections with an elaborate control that takes account of the torque, 'revs', manifold vacuum, and rates of change of these, can cope with this problem, but it is not certain that a simple reliable system can be produced. At the moment, the only system that could guarantee success is the hybrid system in which a low-power economical engine runs at constant speed and charges a battery that can give the surges of power needed for acceleration and be recharged during steady running.

It should be pointed out that, theoretically, it requires no power at all to convey passengers from one point to another at the same height above sea level: all the work of the engine is dissipated in friction: friction in the engine, in the transmission, tyre friction, air friction and in the friction of the brakes, which absorb the kinetic energy of the car when it is stopped. The engine itself can, at best, convert 30-40% of the fuel energy to work, and all this work is itself turned into heat by the friction. It is unlikely that we can raise the engine efficiency substantially, unless we can develop a fuel cell running on air and methanol but mechanical frictional losses can be greatly reduced. Air friction is only serious at high speeds, and it is very doubtful if the private car is a feasible alternative in the future to public transport for long-distance high-speed journeys for safety reasons, fuel economy, economy of drivers' skill, pollution and noise produced per passenger and road space. Probably people will not own cars, but hire them at each end of the journey for the final 10-15 miles from the public-transport station. For the same reasons, the heavy goods lorry will only be used in the future for short-distance (10-50 miles) transport of containers of various sizes from the rail station to the destination.

4 Air pollution from road vehicles

There is, naturally, great controversy as to whether the pollutants from road vehicles are seriously harmful. Table 1 summarises our knowledge of the pollutants. Several of them (CO, Pb, unburnt and partially burnt hydrocarbons, NO_x) have been proved to be poisons to humans, animals and plants when in high enough concentrations. The arguments for continuing to emit these poisons from sources a few centimetres above the ground in ever increasing quantities are mainly based on the measurements of concentrations at levels which are 10^{-1} - 10^{-3} of the levels proved to be lethal. Against these arguments, we have: (a) the commonsense observation of ordinary human beings that they feel uneasy and get headaches when walking in a city street with heavy-vehicle traffic; (b) the occasional occurrence of concentrations that are demonstrably above the danger level; (c) the fact that some of the poisons are known to accummulate on the ground and in water, so that their concentration gradually rises; and (d) clear statistical evidence that certain illnesses are more prevalent and the death rate from others is higher in regions with higher measured pollution levels.

Table 1

Motor vehicle exhaust emissions

Emission	Maximum in exhaust, %	Weight % of fuel	Total weight per year UK x10^6 tons	Total weight per year USA x10^6 tons	Maximum ppm in atmosphere	Notes
CO	10%	25% 15%	5	58	360	Highly toxic 50 parts in 10^6 TLV—2h
C_nH_n	900 parts in 10^6	6%(+2% fuel crankcase c.v. 1½% evap.) wasted	0·25	15·1	15 (5)	Safe limit 500 parts per 10^6
Odour	—	—	—	—	—	Smell unpleasant Carcinogens?
Soot	—	—	—	1·1	—	Dirt & fog. Vehicles 80% of total in USA Diesels
SO_2	—	—	—	0·7 (9)	—	Vehicles 1% of total
Pb	—	0·1% (7)	—	0·18 (7)	44 μg/m^3	200 μgm/m^3 TLV
NO_x	1600 parts in 10^6	2%	0·17	7·3	1·5 parts in 10^6 (5)	Power plants = ½ cars 3 parts in 10^6 for 1h is serious

Lave and Seskin in a classical paper [*Science,* 21st August 1970, 169, (3947), p.723] studied the statistical relationship between various measures of air pollution and human health in 53 country boroughs in the USA. They concluded that:

(a) Air pollution is a significant explanatory variable on the bronchitis death rate in all cases. Unit increase in the particle-deposit index (g/100m^2 - months) leads to an increase of 0·18% in bronchitis mortality rate. The air-pollution variable is extremely important, whereas the socioeconomic variable contributes nothing to the explanatory power.

(b) A 10% decrease in the deposit rate would lead to a 7% decrease in the bronchitis death rate: cleaning the air to the level of the cleanest would lead to a 40% drop in the bronchitis death rate.

(c) The smoke index shows an even stronger correlation with the bronchitis death rate.

(d)   Statistical calculations on lung-cancer data from England and Wales show that 'if the quality of air of all the boroughs was improved to that of the borough with the best air, the rate of death by lung cancer would fall by between 11 and 44%'. A study of white American males (50-69 years old) shows that 'when standardised with respect to both smoking habits and age, the rate of death due to lung cancer was 39 in rural areas and 52 in cities of over 50 000'.

(e)   Another study of lung-cancer deaths of white American males in 46 States showed that the ratio of lung-cancer deaths in urban areas was 1·43 times as high as in rural areas after correcting for both age and smoking history. The rate increased from 1·08 for people who had only lived one year in the towns to 2·0 for lifetime residence.

(f)   'Rates of occurrence of severe respiratory symptoms were 25 – 50% higher for London postmen than for small-town postmen'.

(g)   In London, bus drivers '20 - 35% of absences due to sickness of any kind could be ascribed to air pollution' (measured by a fog index).

(h)   During Asian-flu epidemics, there was a 200% increase in illness in cities with polluted air and only a 20% increase in those with relatively polluted air.

(i)   'For the infant-death rates (ages 28 days to 11 months), the highest concentration was with atmospheric concentrations of SO_3 (mg/100 cm^2 - day), and was 0·70. For the neonatal-death rates (ages 1 day to 27 days) the highest correlation was with dustfall, and was 0·49.'

(j)   Data from 114 standard metropolitan statistical areas in the USA showed that 'a 10% decrease in the minimum concentration of measured particulates would decrease the total death rate by 0·5%. . . . A 10% decrease in the percentage of poor families would decrease the total death rate by 0·2%. . . . A 10% decrease in the minimum concentration of sulphates would decrease the total death rate by 0·4%'.

Lave and Seskin believe that there is conclusive evidence for a substantial quantitative association between air pollution and both mortality and morbidity. They do not attempt to distinguish between the various measures of air pollution, because they have to use whatever measures of air pollution are given in the statistical data. There is little doubt that oxides of sulphur are one of the serious pollutants, and these do not come from vehicles, but are emitted from high chimneys. On the other hand, the particles of lead compounds, the CO and unburnt hydrocarbons and the oxides of nitrogen are emitted from car exhausts and the soot particles from diesel exhausts so close to the ground that the wind velocity is effectively zero, so that a high level of concentration can build up and the particles can be deposited on the road surface and pavements at a dangerously high level. In a traffic jam, these effects, and specially the CO, which can be emitted at rates of up to 10%, can become very serious.

T.J. Chow [Scripps Institute of Oceanography, California, paper to the 2nd international clean-air congress (Academic Press); *New Scientist,* 5th August 1971, p.323] used the measurements of the proportions of the isotopes 204, 206, 207 and 208 of lead to determine the source of lead found in the air and the soil. He showed that the isotopic ratios for pollution lead in ten different cities in Europe, America and Asia correlated very closely with the ratios for the lead in the automobile petrol supplied to the cities: it is concluded that lead in the city air comes almost entirely from petrol and air – the largest single source of human lead. Now it is also known that the mean levels of lead in man, particularly in city children, are nearer the threshold for potential clinical poisoning than is the case for any other environmental pollutant. This is why an outbreak of lead from a factory so quickly causes clinical symptoms. Lead is a cumulative poison in man: it can harm the central nervous system and cause brain damage in children. It is a factor in mental illness, which has been increasing particularly among the young.

In another paper *(Science,* 16th April 1971 Vol. 172 p.265), Hexter and Goldsmith show that there is a significant association between community carbon-monoxide concentrations and mortality. 'The estimated contribution to mortality for an average carbon-monoxide concentration of 20·2 parts in 10^6 (the highest concentration observed during the 4-year period) as compared with an average carbon monoxide concentration of 7·3 parts in 10^6 (the lowest concentration observed) is 11 deaths for that day, all other factors being equal.' They could not find any correlation of oxidant concentration with mortality. The CO is measured as the arithmetic mean of all measurements at all monitoring stations in the Los Angeles air-pollution-control district during a 24 h period. Clearly, the short-term local values in streets would be very much higher, so that the possibility of accidents being caused by the effects of CO on drivers, which would not be shown in this analysis, must be added.

Oxidants (NO_x and O_3) are known to cause eye smarting and damage to plants and rubber, specially under conditions of temperature inversion lasting a week or more: it is the occurrence of these in the Los Angeles basin that has led to the severe US restriction on NO_x emissions from vehicle and stationary combustion systems. However, this lack of correlation of the oxidants with human deaths suggests that we should concentrate our efforts on the elimination of CO and unburnt hydrocarbons.

R.E. Newell ('The global circulation of atmospheric pollutants', *Sci. Amer.,* January 1971, p.32)' states that levels of 50 parts in 10^6 of CO are not uncommon in city streets, with values up to several hundred parts in 10^6 in traffic tunnels and underground garages. 'The toxic effect is proportional to the ambient-air concentration and the time of exposure.

Carbon monoxide that enters the blood stream combines with haemoglobin, forming carboxyhaemoglobin, and thus reduces its capacity to carry oxygen. Impairment of mental function, as measured by visual performance and ability to discriminate time intervals, occur when carboxyhaemoglobin in the blood goes above about 2·5% (compared with a normal level of about 0·5%). Such values accompany exposure to 200 parts in 10^6 for about 15 min or 50 parts in 10^6 for about 2h.

Lead tetraethyl is put into petrol to increase the octane rating in quantities up to 0·1% of the fuel weight (2g/gal = 3·5kg in 'ordinary' petrol, 4g/gal in 'premium'), and 180 000 tons of lead are emitted into the atmosphere every year from the spark-ignition vehicle engines in the USA. It has been calculated that, in the 80 years since this was first used in this way, enough has been emitted to cover every square metre in the USA with 10 mg of lead. It has been suggested that the cause of the observed increase in the lead content of the annually deposited Greenland ice layer is this use of lead in vehicles. Cousteau has stated that the lead in the top 100 m of the sea is now five times what it was 50 years ago.

In a recent paper 'The equations of survival', *(New Scientist,* 1st January 1973, p.482), I have suggested that the concentration C_f of a particular pollutant in the environment is proportional to the product of four factors:

$\frac{N}{A}$ = number of people living in the area A

G_{c+w} = total consumption and wastage of goods averaged per capita in the region

$t_{1/2}$ = half life of the pollutant in the environment, in years; for CO, Newell states that we inject 200 million tons per year from car exhausts into the atmosphere, which would correspond to an increase of 0·03 parts in 10^6 per year — the actual

9

increase is very much less, so that the value of $t_{1/2}$ per CO must be less than 1 year. On the other hand, it has been found that, in the northern hemisphere, where most cars are used, the overall CO concentration is $0·20$ parts in 10^6, but, in the southern, it is only $0·10$ parts in 10^6. CO is absorbed by oxidation to CO_2 in the stratosphere and by microorganism metabolism in the soil — the ocean plays an unknown role. Lead, on the other hand, has a very long dangerous life in the environment, and accumulates in people's nervous systems.

$1/E_1$ = engineering efficiency in getting rid of the pollutant in the system or changing the system to one that does not emit it.

We can do nothing about the first factor, and the world population will rise, and the demand for everyone to have a comparable standard of living will become unavoidable. This makes the problems of improving $1/E_1$ and reducing G_{c+w} in the rich countries urgent and acute. G_{c+w} can be reduced in the present case by using smaller engines, lighter cars, four people in every vehicle, more bicycles and much more public transport.

$1/E_1$ can be improved by:

(a)   raising the exhausts to 6 ft above ground to give more rapid dispersion

(b)   obtaining complete combustion in spark-ignition engines under all conditions to eliminate CO and unburnt hydrocarbons — this also reduces fuel consumption, unlike afterburners and catalytic convertors, which increase fuel consumption and engine size

(c)   changing to diesel engines and running these correctly to avoid soot formation

(d)   use of less polluting fuels such as methane, propane, alcohol, or special mixtures without lead

(e)   use of hybrid ICE — electric systems to eliminate transient problems. These also save fuel and reduce noise, and can save even more fuel if regenerative braking is incorporated.

(f)   use of alternative engines — steam, Stirling or fuel cell.

I must conclude that well before we come to the 21st century we must completely change our attitude towards pollutants - we must regard any pollutant potentially poisonous to humans, animals or plants as guilty until it is proved to be completely innocent at the highest level that can occur and we must change our attitude to the fuel resources of the world to one of caring as much for the needs of our grandchildren as we care for our own. If we do not achieve these changes, we shall achieve disaster before the 21st century reaches the world.

5 Noise

In towns, the vehicle noise comes mainly from the engines, either directly from the cylinders (water-cooled engines are less noisy than air-cooled in this respect), or from the exhaust. Brake squeal, tyre noise, transmission noise and suspension noise are other sources, some being dependent on road bumpiness, others on high speed. Commercial vehicles, specially the largest lorries, are the most unpleasant source of noise, although a badly silenced motorbicycle or sports car can run them close, and even car doors slammed late at night in a quiet neighbourhood can disturb people's sleep. Noise is one of the most neglected causes of the increasing social malaise or enforced fall in the quality of life, and there is no doubt that legal and community action will enforce greatly improved standards.

The Building Research Station interviewed 1400 people living in various relations to roads and expressed dissatisfaction on a scale with a maximum of 7. The best correlation was obtained with a traffic-noise index that measures the difference between the peak noise levels of an individual noisy vehicle and the traffic background averaged over 24 h — a value of TN1 = 102 corresponds to a dissatisfaction of 6, one of TN1 = 70 to a dissatisfaction of 3. Correlation is also close with the peak level averaged over the 18 — 6 a.m. to midnight. L_{10} = 80 dBA corresponds to a dissatisfaction of 6, and 65 dBA to a dissatisfaction of 3.

The ultimate way of reducing the dissatisfaction must be to reduce the peak emissions from vehicles passing by and the general background of the stream of vehicles by quietening the vehicles themselves. The other methods of insulating the buildings against sound, keeping the roads away from the buildings and using noise barriers are, at best, temporary palliatives. A noise barrier with a superficial weight of 10 hg/m^2, with no gaps in it, will reduce the noise level in the shadow area by 20 dBA, which corresponds to a very considerable reduction in dissatisfaction.

11

2   Anti-pollution legislation

P. Draper, F.I.Mech.E., M.Inst.F.
Consultant, UK National Society For Clean Air

The National Society for Clean Air (NSCA) has been pressing for many years for legislation to ensure a reduction in air pollution from the exhausts of motor vehicles of both
the spark-ignition and the compression-ignition engine types. It will be as well to
appreciate why the society has thought this necessary.

As a result of much research by competent organisations, it has been found that neither
the carbon-monoxide and hydrocarbons from petrol engines, nor the smoke from diesel
engines, is at such concentration as to cause real concern regarding animal or vegetable
life; thus why bother to do anything? It is always good amenity policy to reduce the
emission of any air pollutant, provided that it can be done with good reason or at
economic cost and without side effects.

It is well known to engineers and scientists that, since the pollutants with which we are
concerned are the products of incomplete combustion, they can be eliminated or reduced
by ensuring more complete combustion within the engines and thus reducing fuel consumption by an equivalent extent; this should therefore be done, unless the equipment
concerned is too expensive relative to the benefits secured.

The anti-pollution legislation must be considered in two parts, one for the spark-ignition
petrol (gasoline) engine and the other for the compression-ignition (diesel) engine.

1 The spark-ignition engine

It is well known that legislation on this subject started in California, where the peculiar
atmospheric and geographic conditions, which cause air stagnation, and photo-synthesis,
render air pollution a serious problem. Then the idea of severe legislation caught the
imagination of the American public and politicians, with the unfortunate result that
savage Federal legislation has been enacted quite out of proportion to the trouble that
it has been designed to correct. This legislation is causing the expenditure of many
millions of dollars and other currencies in an attempt to meet it by the deadline date
of 1976; furthermore, the devices that are being designed to treat the exhaust gases
between the engine and the tail pipe will cause appreciably higher running costs and
constant maintenance attention. In fact, it seems unlikely that even frequent attention
will enable the devices to control the emissions after a period of operation.

There is no need to set out the full details of the US legislation, which has been modified and reported many times. The latest summary appears in Table 1.

Table 1

US Federal motor-vehicle emission standards, gal/mile

	1971	1972	1973	1974	1975	1976
HC	4·1	3·0	3·0	3·0	0·41	0·41
CO	34·0	28·0	28·0	28·0	3·4	3·4
NO_x	–	–	3·1	3·1	3·1	0·4

It will be seen that a modification now defines the pollution limits in grams per mile, instead of the earlier percentage of volume of the exhaust gases. This later scale would appear to penalise larger vehicles.

On studying the literature, it is found that almost every country of the world is forming its own pollution limits, so that the subject is becoming very complex. In Europe alone, the countries are not in agreement, but the British regulation, which was announced in December 1973, requires that petrol-engined vehicles first used after November 1973 shall comply with the limits for the emission of CO and HC_s laid down by the Economic Commission for Europe Report 15. It is claimed that this will reduce emission of CO by up to 30% and HC by up to 10%. This will be achieved by better carburation and spark devices.

The actual tests prescribed by the ECE Regulation 15 requires that the car shall be tested on a chassis dynamometer by a cycle of conditions representing driving in a congested urban area after a cold start. Fig. 1 shows the approximate cycle conditions. The exhaust gases will be collected in a plastic bag for overall analysis. The maximum permissible mass of CO and HC_s are set out as in Table 2, relating them to the weight of the vehicle concerned.

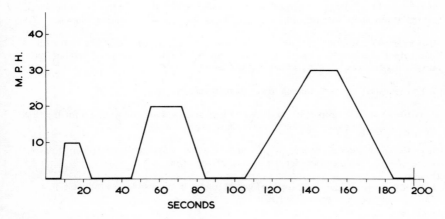

Fig. 1   E.C.E. test cycle

Table 2

ECE Regulation 15. Emission limits as function of vehicle weight.

Weight of Vehicle kg up to	750	850	1020	1250	1470	1700	1930	2150	and over
CO, g/test *	100	109	117	134	152	167	186	203	220
HC_s, g/test *		8·0	8·4	8·7	9·4	10·1	10·8	11·4	14·1	12·8

* The ECE test-cycle equivalent to 4·05 km (2·54 miles)

A second test that will be carried out on new vehicles will be the measurement of the percentage of carbon monoxide at idling speed with a hot engine. The volume of CO content of the exhaust gases must not exceed 4·5%.

My own comment here is that these regulations are satisfactory but rather overcautious. I believe that better attention to carburation may well reduce CO emissions by an average of 60%. I also hazard a guess that the hot-idling test will be found adequate for the checking of cars the prototypes of which have undergone the full chassis dynamometer test.

Since the 1st January 1972, all cars are required to be fitted with a device for recycling crankcase emissions.

The UK Department of the Environment has recently announced a phased programme to reduce the lead content of petrol. The maximum permitted level will be cut by almost one-half over the next three years. The present permitted maximum is 0·84 g/l, which was to be reduced to 0·64 g/l by the end of 1972, to 0·55 g/l by the end of 1973, and to 0·45 g/l by the end of 1975.

The amount of lead currently added to 5-star petrols is less than the present permitted maximum, and there is no medical or other evidence that the quantity of lead emitted to the atmosphere is significant with that provided by nature and other sources.

The proposed reduction of lead additive in petrols seems to be acceptable to the oil companies who have to produce the petrol, and is acceptable all round provided that no further reduction is contemplated, the reasons being that

(a)   the lower limit is not much lower than current practice

(b)   the antiknock properties produced by lead additives are considerable for the first small additions but further amounts have progressively less effect

(c)   the small quantity of lead permitted by the regulations will be sufficient to avoid valve-seat sinkage experienced with leadfree petrol

(d)   any less lead than that proposed would render it impossible to produce 5-star petrol except at prohibitive cost

(e)   any less lead, or a leadfree petrol, would entail the lowering of the compression ratios of current high-performance cars with consequent increase of fuel consumption, thus adding even further cost to motoring.

Summing up, the reduction of lead emissions for amenity reasons is acceptable at the proposed level, as the extra cost will not be much, but any further reduction would rapidly render the cost unjustifiable.

2 The compression-ignition engine (diesel)

The problem with this form of engine is one of smoke emission only. The other products of partial combustion are negligible.

Legislation has also been enacted recently to take care of this problem. The most important regulation (Regulation 25B) requires that, after the 1st April 1973, a compression-ignition (c.i.) engine shall be so constructed that it complies with the British Standard AU 141a for the maximum capacity of smoke emitted at all loads. This would be entirely satisfactory if the BS AU 141a smoke limits were acceptable, but, in the view of the NSCA, this is not so. I will explain:

Fig. 2 shows when a c.i. engine smokes and postulates a maximum smoke level that would be acceptable to the NSCA, and the public in general. Such a level, though less than visible, can be recorded on the scales of the Hartridge and Bosch smoke meters; it would provide a reasonable margin to take care of the slight increase in smoke level that always occurs as a vehicle builds up its milage on the road.

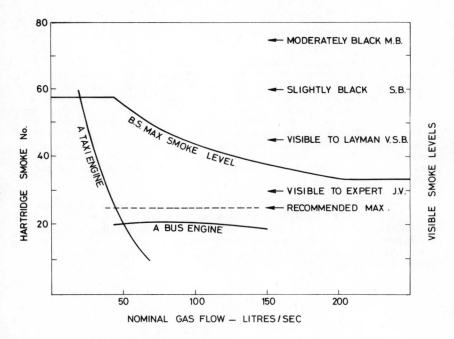

Fig. 2   BS maximum smoke level

Fig. 3 shows the BSAU 141a maximum smoke levels proposed for the whole range of engine throughputs, which covers all sizes of vehicle engine, as well as full throttle part loads at reduced engine revolutions per minute.

The recommended maximum level shown in Fig. 2 is shown by the dotted line.

15

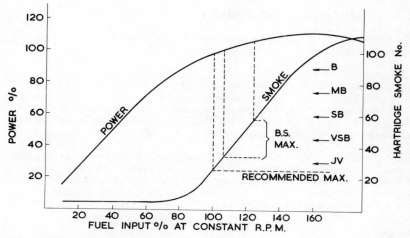

Fig. 3   Effect of fuel input on power and smoke

The most obvious feature of the BS curve is that it permits much higher smoke intensity — well into the visible range — for smaller engines, or at lower rev/min of larger engines — the reason claimed for this apparent anomaly being that, since the volume of exhaust gases from smaller engines is less than from larger ones, the smoke plume is not as objectionable as is, judged by eye. I regard this as begging the question, and can see no reason why, say, ten taxis should be permitted to emit much more visible smoke than one bus. Of course, there is another reason that prompted the BS limits, namely that small c.i. engines operating at low rev/min do tend to smoke more. The technical answer is to improve the combustion efficiency of such engines at reduced rev/min or to cause them to operate at higher 'revs', or to fit larger engines more capable of the duty required of them.

In conclusion, I suggest that we must be pleased that reasonable legislation is at last enacted to ensure that air pollution from all British vehicles of both types is to be controlled by law. It is to be hoped, and likely to come about, that the regulations will be modified in the light of experience; but it is also hoped that we will not be steamrollered into adopting the unrealistic US Federal regulations other than for export-market purposes.

16

Part 2

Non-steady internal combustion engines

3 The spark-ignition reciprocating gasoline engine

D. Collins
Ricardo & Co., Engineers (1927) Ltd., Shoreham by Sea, Sussex, England

1 Introduction

This paper reviews the present situation and feasibility of meeting the 1975-76 US
Federal emission limits by using a spark-ignited, reciprocating gasoline engine. A
report published in the USA by the National Academy of Sciences (Reference 1) to the
Committee on Motor Vehicle Emissions to Congress and to the Environmental
Protection Agency, stated that, at present, four engine types will meet the 1975
certification standards and could be mass-produced in sufficient quantity to meet the
1975 market demand. These engines were:

(a) the modified conventional engine equipped with an oxidation catalyst

(b) the carburetted stratified-charge engine

(c) the Wankel rotary engine equipped with an exhaust thermal reactor

(d) the diesel engine

This report also stated that, at present, five emission-control systems had been developed
that met the 1976 standards, these being four versions of the conventional engine
employing combinations of catalysts, thermal reactors and fuel injection, and the
stratified-charge engine equipped with fuel injection and a catalyst.

However, almost all the systems had failed after a few thousand miles, and the selection
of engines certifiable for 1976 may not be sufficiently mass-producible to satisfy the
expected demand. The most promising system, at present being evaluated, was the
dual-carburetted stratified charge engine developed in Japan. The report also expressed
concern about the direction of emission-control development taken by most manufacturers, stating 'the system most likely to be available in 1976 in the greatest numbers —
the dual-catalyst system — was the most disadvantageous with respect to first cost, fuel
economy, maintainability and durability'.

Having painted a rather gloomy picture for the future of the conventional automotive
power plant, I will attempt to describe the various modifications and additions that can
be applied to it to make it comply with the US emission regulations. The two possible
alternative power plants mentioned in the report, the Wankel and the diesel will be
dealt with in detail by later speakers.

US Federal emission-test procedures and limits

Before describing the engine modifications required, it is worth briefly reviewing the
limits and the test methods by which they are measured. Fig. 1 shows how, for 1975,

the hydrocarbon and carbon-monoxide limits, and, for 1976, the nitrogen oxide limits, are to be drastically reduced. These values were finally fixed in January 1972 after many delays, and were as follows:

		g/mile
1975	HC	0·41
	CO	3·40
	NO_x	3·10
1976	HC	0·41
	CO	3·40
	NO_x	0·40

Year	Standard	Cold Start Test	Hydrocarbons	Carbon monoxide	Oxides of Nitrogen
1970	State & Federal	7-mode	2.2 gm/mi	23 gm/mi	no std.
1971	State	7-mode	2.2 gm/mi	23 gm/mi	4 gm/mi
	Federal	7-mode	2.2 gm/mi	23 gm/mi	-
1972	State	7-mode or CVS-1	1.5 gm/mi 3.2 gm/mi	23 gm/mi 39 gm/mi	3 gm/mi
	Federal	CVS-1	3.4 gm/mi	39 gm/mi	-
1973	State	CVS-1	3.2 gm/mi	39 gm/mi	3 gm/mi
	Federal	CVS-1	3.4 gm/mi	39 gm/mi	3 gm/mi
1974	State	CVS-1	3.2 gm/mi	39 gm/mi	2 gm/mi
	Federal	CVS-1	3.4 gm/mi	39 gm/mi	3 gm/mi
1975	State	CVS-1	1 gm/mi	24 gm/mi	1.5 gm/mi
	Federal	CVS-2	0.41 gm/mi	3.4 gm/mi	3.1 gm/mi
1976	State	CVS-1	1 gm/mi	24 gm/mi	1.5 gm/mi
	Federal	CVS-2	0.41 gm/mi	3.4 gm/mi	0.4 gm/mi

Fig. 1   US gasoline emission standards for light-duty vehicles under 6000 lb

For the purpose of this paper, the alternative limits either applied for, or granted to, the California Air Resources Board have been neglected, although they are hoping for a lower NO_x level than the Federal limit in 1975. This left very little lead time for the manufacturers to obtain the necessary technology and hardware to meet these limits, although most had feared the worst for some time previous to the finalised limits being published, and had been actively engaged in research towards meeting them. However, the indecision about the test procedure and exact limits had led to some misdirected efforts. An application by some motor manufacturers, both European and American, to have the 1975 limits postponed for a year was rejected by the Environmental Protection Agency (EPA), but there are still hopes that the 1976 emission limits will be postponed for a year owing to the greater problem experienced when trying to reduce the three main pollutants simultaneously.

19

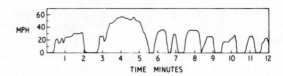

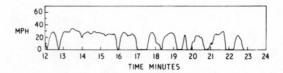

Fig. 2　　1972 CVS test cycle

The test method employed to measure the emissions requires the vehicle to be driven on a chassis dynamometer, over a 7·5 mile 23 min non-repetitive cycle, known as the LA 4 (Fig. 2). The vehicle is then allowed to stand for 10 min before driving the first 505 of the cycle again. This means that the test includes a cold and hot start, although, prior to the cold start, the vehicle has been stored in the test area, which has to be controlled between 60 and 86°F. During the driving cycle, the total vehicle exhaust is fed into a constant volume sampler (CVS) (Fig. 3), which consists of a blower passing a constant volume of air that variably dilutes the exhaust gas to give a true mass emission value. A small sample of this diluted exhaust is continuously pumped into a sample bag, which is analysed for HC, CO and NO_x following completion of the test. The test is divided into three parts, known as the cold-transient, stabilised and hot-transient phases, and a separate sample bag is filled during each of these. Following the bag analysis, a relatively simple calculation is carried out taking into account factors such as the volume of dilution air, its temperature, pressure and humidity, the density of the three pollutants and the distance driven. A weighting factor is applied to reduce the influence of the cold-start emissions on the final answer. This describes briefly the test procedure, which is laid down in very great detail in a lengthy legal document.

2 Conventional engines

This part of the paper will deal with the various hang-on devices that can be applied to the spark-ignited engine to reduce its emission levels.

2.1 Oxidising catalysts

The use of an oxidising catalyst to reduce HC and CO emission levels is one of the most favoured methods of meeting the 1975 US Federal limits. These catalysts can be of the base-metal, copper-oxide, vanadium-pentoxide or noble-metal type, such as platinum, paladium etc., and operate by converting the HC and CO into H_2O and CO_2 in the presence of excess O_2. The catalyst is applied to a support that requires a large surface-area/volume ratio, and these are mainly of the ceramic-matrix or alumina-pellet/granule type. This is contained in a specially designed casing to give good gas distribution, without causing excessive back pressure. It has to be mounted in such a position in the exhaust system that it warms up quickly, as the emission test commences from the initial cranking of the engine and any exhaust that passes the catalyst before it has reached its operating temperature will heavily influence the overall result. The mixture-strength range with which the oxidising catalyst can cope is not very critical, and extra air is added to the exhaust

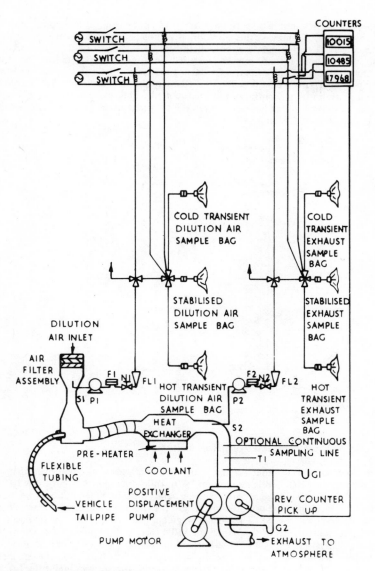

Fig. 3 Ricardo exhaust gas sampling system

stream after it leaves the engine, to provide an excess of O_2 for complete oxidation. This secondary air supply, as it is known, is provided by an engine-driven pump. The mixture-strength requirement can be obtained with the present-day type of sophisticated emission carburettor, but some manufacturers favour the use of fuel-injection systems, mainly electronic. However, as the catalytic reaction is exothermic, it is important to avoid overrich mixtures, as the heat produced can cause damage to the catalyst itself or its support material. Promising results have been obtained with promoted platinum catalysts applied to a ceramic matrix, such as are sold by Engelhard and Johnson Matthey (Fig. 4). The platinum catalyst has an advantage in its low initial lightoff temperature resistance, although it is still possible to exceed the permitted maximum

21

temperature in the event of a spark-plug failure when the catalyst is supplied with an overrich mixture. To prevent this situation, it will be necessary to have some warning to sense catalyst overtemperature, but whether an audible and/or visible warning will be sufficient or some form of bypass device will be allowed is not yet clear. Another problem with the majority of present oxidising catalysts is the effect on them of the lead in petrol. To overcome this, the US Federal authorities have specified maximum lead and phosphorus concentrations in the fuel that will be available from 1975 onwards, but, even at these low lead levels, some durability problems are being experienced owing to lead poisoning of the catalyst.

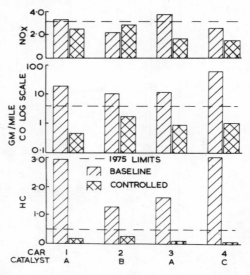

Fig. 4   1975 CVS test results

2.1 Dual bed, reduction and oxidation, catalysts

The dual-bed-catalyst approach is one of the main methods so far developed that will meet the very low NO_x levels required in 1976 while still maintaining the low HC and CO levels of the previous year. The reducing catalyst itself, which converts NO into N_2 and O_2, can be either base or noble metal, and the support again either ceramic matrix or alumina granules (Fig. 5). The system when applied to a vehicle consists of a reducing catalyst, for control of nitrogen oxides mounted close to the engine, followed by an oxidising catalyst for HC and CO as described in Section 1 (Fig. 6). The positioning of the catalysts is important, as the reducing box must be close enough to the engine to warmup quickly, but far enough away to avoid overheating at least under the LA 4 driving cycle conditions. As the oxidising catalyst has to be positioned downstream of the reducing box, its ability to operate from low temperatures is important. In some applications, both catalysts are fitted in the same container to reduce the metal mass and therefore give faster warmup. Another method of improving warmup is to use the reducing catalyst for oxidising during the initial part of the test. This means that excess O_2 is applied to it and an oxidising reaction occurs that commences at a lower temperature and warms up the catalyst. The NO_x levels are generally low during this period, as the choke is in operation and the mixture strength supplied to the engine is overrich. Once the reducing bed has reached its lightoff temperature, the air supply is diverted to the oxidising catalyst, which has already been warmed by the exhaust gas passing through it. The mixture-strength requirement of the reducing catalyst, however, is very critical, and it is important to maintain an O_2 level of less than 0·5% to obtain

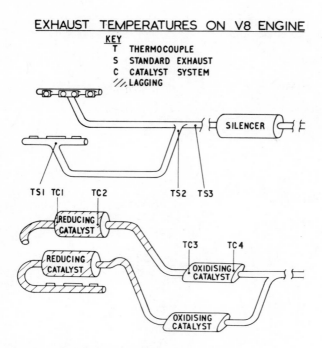

EXHAUST TEMPERATURES ON V8 ENGINE

SILENCER

TS1   TC1   TC2   TS2   TS3

REDUCING CATALYST

REDUCING CATALYST

TC3   TC4

OXIDISING CATALYST

OXIDISING CATALYST

Fig. 5   Exhaust temperatures on V8 engine

the optimum reducing activity, because, if a higher level of O_2 is present, the reducing catalyst becomes oxidised. However, the minimum richness to obtain this O_2 level must be used; otherwise the hydrogen in the exhaust reacts over the reducing catalyst to produce ammonia, NH_3. This ammonia is then reconverted to NO_x over the oxidising ca catalyst, so lowering the overall NO_x conversion efficiency. This critical mixture-strength requirement is very difficult to maintain with existing carburettors, and favours the use of a fuel-injection system, preferably with a closed-loop control system, which will be described in detail later.

To allow the 1976 NO_x levels to be obtained, it is necessary on some vehicles to apply exhaust-gas recirculation to reduce the levels leaving the engine. By using this in addition to a reducing catalyst, it has been possible to reduce the NO_x levels below the legal limits. Although results below the 1976 limits can be obtained (Fig. 7), these are at zero-mile conditions only, and the durability of such catalyst systems at present is very poor.

2.3 Exhaust-gas recirculation (EGR)

A method of reducing nitrogen-oxide levels in the cylinder of an engine is to recycle exhaust gas either internally, by the use of suitable valve timings, or externally by a controlled bleed from the exhaust to the inlet manifold. The inert gas thus induced lowers the combustion efficiency and peak cylinder temperatures, and hence reduces the production of nitrogen oxides within the cylinder. For 1975 models, this system can be applied in conjunction with the oxidising-catalyst approach if the engine base-line levels are above the limit, as a 50% reduction in nitrogen-oxide levels can be obtained without too much effect on vehicle driveability. The use of EGR usually results in higher HC emissions from the engine, due to reduced combustion efficiency, and a worsening of fuel consumption. When external EGR is used to trim emission

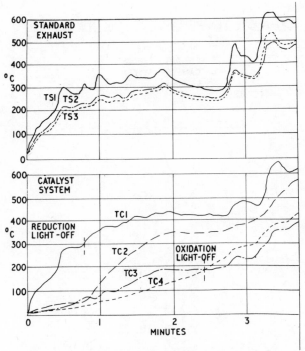

Fig. 6   Exhaust temperatures during CVS test

levels, it can be controlled by a fairly simple vacuum-operated valve, but, as the amount of NO_x reduction required increases more complex methods of control are required to avoid problems with the driveability and to ensure that the optimum quantity to obtain the desired reduction is recycled. It seems unlikely that the 1976 emission levels will be met by the use of EGR in conjunction with an oxidising catalyst only, as Fig. 8 shows that the best results that could be obtained using very complex control of EGR, carburation and secondary-air-injection quantities did not quite meet the NO_x levels. There was a considerable penalty in fuel consumption, although the driveability was still acceptable. EGR will be required on some engines to meet the 1976 levels even with a dual catalyst system, since, as at present, the reduction catalysts are not capable of overall conversion efficiencies of much greater than 90%. If the prototype emission levels are set at 50% of the legal limits, i.e. 0·2 g/mile NO_x, a typical value used by the motor manufacturers, then the vehicle baseline level of NO_x must not exceed 2·0 g/mile. This value is exceeded by many vehicles emphasising the necessity of EGR as an addition to the reducing catalyst until its conversion efficiency can be considerably improved. Although the application of EGR itself does not affect the engine's fuel requirement, the use of leadfree fuels is advantageous to the EGR system as they reduced blockages and pipe fouling due to combustion deposits.

2.4   Exhaust-manifold thermal reactors

Much development work has been carried out on the thermal reactor as a possible means of reducing HC and CO levels. The reactor consists of a large-volume exhaust manifold into which air is injected. By restricting the flow of the exhaust and increasing its residence time in the manifold, very high temperatures can be attained, which result in oxidation of the HC and CO leaving the engine, without affecting the NO_x levels. This

24

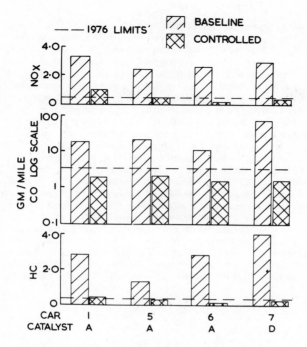

Fig. 7   1976 CVS test results

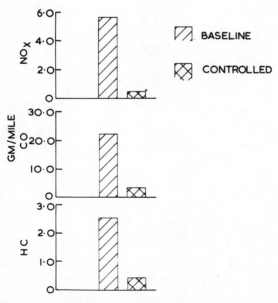

Fig. 8   1975 CVS test result on optimised emission-control system

25

means that some alternative method of NO_x control, such as EGR has to be used in conjunction with it. As with the catalytic convertor, the warmup rate is very important, and insulation is usually fitted to improve this and reduce the external-skin temperatures that can result in very high underbonnet temperatures. The high internal temperatures attained require the use of high-quality materials to avoid thermal failure, and ceramics are being used in some applications to overcome the many difficulties being experienced. Tests carried out by Ricardo on a European-size vehicle fitted with a thermal reactor and timed air injection, to improve reactor efficiency, are shown in Fig. 9. No external NO_x control was applied, as the target was the 1975 levels, but the reduction in levels from the baseline was due in part to the richer mixture required to obtain maximum reactor efficiency. It was not possible to obtain sufficient oxidation of the carbon monoxide, a problem that has been experienced by other people using thermal reactors, although the HC levels could be reduced to approximately 50% of the limit. When the vehicle was tested to the ISO R362 noise test, it showed a reduction of 4 dB, but suffered a considerable loss in performance and worsening of the fuel consumption. The loss of performance was due, not only to an increase in exhaust back pressure, but to the fact that the reactor manifold replaced an extractor-type exhaust manifold used to obtain a good engine performance, a quite common design feature on European-sized vehicles. The Du Pont Company has been one of the major exponents of the thermal reactor for some years because of its ability to accept leaded fuels without ill effect, unlike the catalytic convertor. Tests on vehicles fitted with their latest thermal reactor and using exhaust-gas recirculation rates of up to 24% give (Reference 4) emission levels of

	g/mile
HC	0·09
CO	4·50
NO_x	0·32

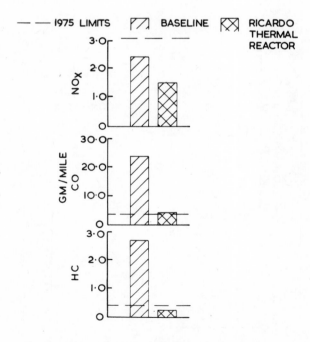

Fig. 9   1975 CVS test results (car 9)

26

showing again that, although the HC and NO_x limits were reached, the CO limit was not. Work is continuing to overcome this problem of CO conversion in thermal reactors, but, at present, the only application that appears to be capable of reaching the CO limits is the Wankel rotary engine, and this has a higher exhaust temperature than the recipro-cating engine, which is an important factor in obtaining good CO conversion.

An interesting system has been developed by the Questor Automotive Product Co., in the USA, called the Questor Reverter, which is a combination of thermal reactor and catalyst. The exhaust manifold of the engine is replaced by a simple small-volume thermal reactor into which a limited quantity of air is injected. This oxidises some of the HC and CO, increases the exhaust temperature, but maintains a CO-rich atmosphere. The gas then passes into the postmanifold reverter containing thin expanded Inconel 601 grids plated with copper, which act as reducing catalysts for the NO_x. Further secondary air is injected downstream of the catalyst grids, and oxidation of the remaining CO and HC is carried out. To increase the temperature of the injected air and to prevent the exhaust pipes from becoming excessively hot, the secondary air is passed along a length of double-skinned exhaust pipe in the opposite direction to the exhaust gas flow. To date, the lowest zero-mile emission levels obtained with this system fitted to a 400 in^3 V8 engine have been

	g/mile
HC	0·07
CO	2·80
NO_x	0·25

It is claimed to be unaffected by leaded fuels, but the fuel consumption is 15% worse than a typical 1973 model of similar engine capacity.

2.5 Single-bed dual-function catalysts

The mixture-strength requirements of both a single oxidising catalyst and the separate reducing and oxidising catalyst systems are such that it is not essential to use fuel injection, although, in some cases, this is favoured, as its better mixture distribution results in lower base-line-emission levels from the engine. However, the single-bed dual-function catalyst, in which both NO_x reduction and HC and CO oxidation occur over the same catalyst, has such a critical range of mixture strength over which it will function that a closed-loop electronic fuel-injection system is essential (Fig. 10).
To obtain conversion efficiencies of 90-95% of all three emissions, the air/fuel ratio must be maintained within ± 0·1 ratios of stoichiometric. This close control is obtained by using an oxygen sensor in the exhaust upstream of the catalyst, which feeds back information to the electronic fuel-injection control system and alters the mixture strength accordingly. The oxygen sensor can utilise zirconium dioxide in a hollow cylindrical tube closed at one end. The outside of the tube is exposed to the exhaust gas, and the inside of the tube is referenced to atmospheric oxygen, with the zirconium dioxide acting as a solid electrolyte. All the inside and outside surfaces are coated with platinum, which serves as a catalyst and provides conductive electrodes to sense the electric poten-tial produced by the sensor (Fig. 11). These sensors have unique switch-like character-istics over the air/fuel ratio range in which these dual-function catalysts operate, and the potential produced varies rapidly as the oxygen level in the exhaust alters. The Bendix Corporation (Reference 5) has developed a closed-loop injection system, which, when tested on a 2500 lb 4-cylinder vehicle fitted with 5% exhaust-gas recirculation and a dual-function catalyst, but no secondary airpump, gave an average result of

	g/mile
HC	0·18
CO	2·50
NO_x	0·23

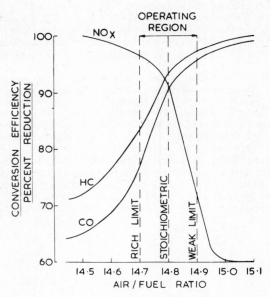

Fig. 10 Dual-function catalyst characteristics

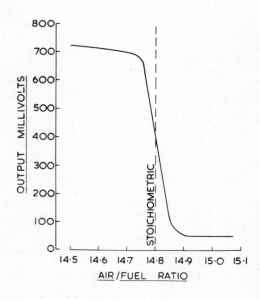

Fig. 11 Oxygen sensor characteristics

28

These results were obtained at zero milage, and the durability of the oxygen sensor is as yet unknown, but this system does provide an attractive, if somewhat complex, solution to the problem. However, the use of a catalyst will result in a leadfree fuel requirement, although the economy and driveability of this system should not be impaired as much as with some other systems, as it maintains a constant mixture strength under all driving conditions.

2.6 The 2-stroke engine

Although the introduction of the early emission limits in the USA was one of the reasons for the withdrawal of a 2-stroke-engined car sold there, there are signs now that this engine is being reconsidered along with other alternative power plants as a possible solution to the 1975-76 emission limits. Suzuki, the Japanese motor-cycle manufacturer, has produced a system called EPIC, exhaust-port ignition cleaner, which is claimed to have produced emission levels below the 1976 limits when tested in a car with a 360 cc engine. This system consists of air injection into the exhaust and an igniter to promote afterburning to oxidise HC and CO. The 2-stroke-engine has a low basic NO_x level and therefore offers an immediate advantage over the 4-stroke. Ricardo has carried out some bench tests on a twin-cylinder 2-stroke engine with crankcase compression fitted with an oxidising catalyst. The results of these tests are shown in Fig. 12. Although the uncontrolled emissions were high, there was sufficient oxygen in the exhaust to allow the HC levels to be reduced greatly without the use of air injection at part and full load and the CO levels at part load. However, the CO emissions were not reduced at full load until extra air was supplied. The lower efficiency of the catalyst at part load even with air injection was due to low exhaust-gas temperatures. Problems were experienced with the drop in performance owing to the increased exhaust backpressure, the deposition of soot on the catalyst and mechanical deterioration of the

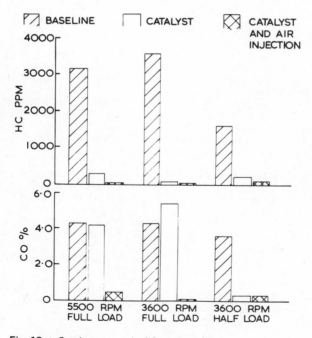

Fig. 12 Catalyst control of 2-stroke engine

29

catalyst support. In spite of these problems, there is evidence to suggest that a sophisticated 2-stroke engine using fuel injection, an external blower and conventional 4-stroke lubrication system could provide an alternative power plant.

3. Unconventional engines

As far as this paper is concerned, the term 'unconventional' refers to modifications to the reciprocating engine that are intended to reduce its baseline-emission levels. One form of power plant that has been receiving considerable attention recently is the carburetted stratified-charge engine, which has been shown to be capable of meeting the 1975 US Federal limits without any hang-on devices at all.

3.1 Prechamber stratified charge

The most recent development of this type of engine has come from the Japanese Honda Motor Co. in the form of its CVCC engine, the initials standing for 'compound vortex controlled combustion', which utilises a small prechamber with its own inlet valve.
A rich mixture is drawn into the prechamber, and a very weak mixture is drawn into the main combustion space through the conventional inlet valve. The spark plug ignites the rich mixture, which then leaves the prechamber and burns the weak-mixture portion of the charge. This form of combustion lowers the peak temperatures, which prevents the formation of NO_x, but maintains a temperature sufficiently high to oxidise the hydrocarbons and provides a mixture lean enough to oxidise the carbon monoxide.
This type of engine has been tested by the EPA, and one of the engines that had previously been driven for 50 000 miles recorded an average emission level of

	g/mile
HC	0·18
CO	2·12
NO_x	0·89

which is well inside the 1975 limits. The fuel consumption of this engine, when tested in a 2000 lb Civic vehicle, was 20% lower than the average of the 1973 2000 lb certification vehicles, and Honda admits that the fuel consumption of the CVCC engine is 10% worse than the conventional engine used in their Civic model. An advantage of the system is that it will operate on leaded petrol, as there is no catalyst to poison, although the 50 000 mile test was run on leadfree fuel to prove the durability of the 3-valve layout. However, the penalty for the low emissions is the low specific output of the engine: 65 hp from a 2 litre engine, 32½ hp/litre.

In its present form, the CVCC engine does not meet the 1976 limits on account of its NO_x emissions, but Honda appear confident that these can be reduced further, but whether this can be accomplished by mixture variations or the use of exhaust-gas recirculation is not known. Incidentally, in 1915, Sir Harry Ricardo filed a patent application for a stratified-charge engine incorporating a prechamber with its own valve, and apart from this valve being automatic, the mode of operation is very similar to that employed by Honda. However, the intention of this engine was to enable a high compression ratio to be used without detonation occurring, as, at that time, exhaust emissions were not attracting much attention.

3.2 Fuel-injected stratified charge

A considerable amount of work has been carried out on this type of engine, the most well known being the Ford PROCO (programmed combustion process) and Texaco TCCS (Texaco-controlled combustion system).

(a) Ford PROCO

This engine is the second generation of the Ford-combustion-process (FCP) engine, which has been developed with the intention of obtaining low emission levels with the minimum loss of fuel economy. To obtain this, it has been necessary to use air throttling and exhaust-gas recirculation in addition to fuel injection. The system has been applied to the military L141 engine, which has been fitted in an M151 ¼ ton utility truck. Instead of using a prechamber as in the Honda CVCC system, the combustion chamber is formed in the piston crown. A high swirl rate of 3 to 5 times the crankshaft speed is induced, and the compression ratio is 11:1. A low-penetration wide-angle spray injector positioned near the centre line of the cylinder bore injects a rich mixture into the centre of the chamber, surrounded by a leaner mixture and excess air. The spark plug initiates rapid combustion in the rich mixture, which spreads to the leaner regions, flame travel being promoted by the intake swirl and toroidal movement imparted by the squish action. As the piston moves down its stroke, the charge expands out of the combustion chamber, and the air motion homogenises the mixture to promote complete combustion. However, the emissions from this engine are well above the 1975 or 1976 emission levels, although an improvement in fuel consumption and emission levels over the original FCP engine was obtained. By using exhaust-gas recirculation and an oxidising catalyst, requiring leadfree fuel, the emission levels (Reference 2) have been reduced to

	g/mile
HC	0·37
CO	0·93
NO_x	0·33

There is sufficient excess O_2 in the exhaust of this type of engine to allow the oxidising catalyst to operate without the need for a secondary air-injection pump. This system can therefore reach the 1976 emission levels at zero miles, but durability information is not yet available, and some of the present design features are not considered feasible for volume production.

(b) Texaco TCCS

This system has also been applied to the military L141 engine, and is similar to the Ford PROCO system in that the combustion chamber is formed in the piston. A high swirl rate within the cylinder is generated with the aid of a masked inlet valve and the fuel-injector and spark-plug relative positions are carefully controlled. The fuel is injected tangentially to the air swirl and directed at the spark plug. By careful optimisation of the injection and ignition timing, combustion is initiated as the fuel reaches the spark plug, and the flame front then remains stationary as the swirling air brings more fuel to maintain the combustion patch at its critical size. Good mixing of fuel and air in conjunction with the long-duration ignition provided by the transistorised system results in complete combustion and reduces the emission levels considerably, compared with the standard L141 engine. However, to approach the 1976 emission levels, it is necessary to apply exhaust-gas recirculation, and an oxidation catalyst, and, when tested in this form, the following result (Reference 3) was obtained

	g/mile
HC	0·89
CO	1·46
NO_x	0·38

This result did not meet the HC levels, and further development work has been carried out; the engine has now met the 1976 limits for all three emissions, and continued to do so for 50 000 miles. Because of the use of an oxidation catalyst, a leadfree fuel is required, and the fuel consumption is claimed to be better than the basic L141 engine, but this engine was not renowned for good economy.

4. Summary

This paper has attempted to review the present state of development of the reciprocating engine towards meeting the 1975-76 US Federal emission levels, and indicated that considerable effort is being made, although most of the solutions result in a reduction in fuel economy. How long this will be allowed to continue is a matter for conjecture, as the latest interest appears to be conservation of the rapidly diminishing fuel reserves of the world. Whether the drastic reduction of emission levels is justified if it results in poorer fuel consumptions is a matter for the US Government to decide, but at present, it appears that the two factors are inseparable.

5. Acknowledgments

The author wishes to thank his colleagues responsible for the tests summarised in this paper and also the Directors of Ricardo & Co. for permission to publish it.

6. Addendum

Since this paper was originally written, the one-year postponement of the 1975 limits requested by four US manufacturers, namely General Motors, Ford, Chrysler and International Harvester, has been granted. This has resulted in 'interim' 1975 standards being set, which are as follows:

California only:

	g/mile
HC	0·9
CO	9·0
NO_x	2.0

US Federal

	g/mile
HC	1·5
CO	15·0
NO_x	3·1

The 1976 standards are also being reviewed as far as NO_x levels are concerned, and it seems likely that the level of 0·4 g/mile will be relaxed considerably. It is not immediately possible to judge the impact of these changes on the developments described in this paper, except that the stratified-charge engine, such as the Honda CVCC, which does not require any hang-on devices, seems an even more attractive solution to the confirmed 1975, and suggested 1976, revised limits.

References

1   National Research Council, Committee on Motor Vehicle Emissions, Report on feasibility of auto emission control systems, 12th December 1973

2   SIMKO, A., CHOMA M.A. and REPKO, L.L.: 'Exhaust emission control by the Ford programmed combustion process — PROCO' SAE 730052

3   MITCHELL, E., ALPERSTEIN, M., COBB J.M. and FAIST C.J.,: 'A stratified charge multi-fuel military engine — a progress report'. SAE 720510

4   CANTWELL E.N., HOFFMAN R.A., ROSENLUND I.T., and ROSS S.W,: 'A systems approach to vehicle emission control'. SAE 72051

5   RIVARD J.G.,: 'Closed-loop electronic fuel injection control of the internal combustion engine'. SAE 73005

4 The reciprocating diesel engine

C.J. Walder, C.Eng., F.I.Mech.E.
D. Broome, M.A., C.Eng., M.I.Mech.E.
P.S.J. Ritchie, C.Eng., M.I.Mech.E.
Ricardo & Co., Engineers (1927) Ltd., Shoreham by Sea, Sussex, England.

1   Introduction

Although regulations affecting the emissions of internal combustion engines have been in force in Europe for more than 45 years in regard to their use in mines, it was not until the upsurge of interest and concern for the environment in the mid-1960s that attention was focused on the emissions characteristics of the diesel engine. The introduction of legislation by the Californian Air Resources Board affecting the specific emissions of hydrocarbons, oxides of nitrogen and carbon monoxide, as well as visible smoke for on-highway vehicles powered by diesel engines, has presented challenging targets to all engine manufacturers. In efforts to meet the severe limits proposed for 1975 and beyond, it has been necessary to take a critical look at the emission characteristics of all types of combustion chamber and to evaluate the effect of engine, injection and other variables on these characteristics. Numerous papers reporting on such investigations have already been presented to various societies (e.g. References 1, 2 and 3), and this paper is a further contribution covering the practical work that has been carried out by Ricardo in their laboratories at Shoreham by Sea, England. This work, together with theoretical studies, is still continuing, and such is the progress that is being made today in the field of emissions that this paper must be regarded as being an interim report and by no means the final word.

2   Current legislation

Currently the only enacted or proposed legislation covering invisible exhaust emissions from heavy-duty diesel engines for on-highway applications concerns the USA. Such legislation covers the pollutants carbon monoxide, hydrocarbons and oxides of nitrogen. The State of California, through its Air Resources Board (CARB) was the first to promulgate such regulations, involving a hot-engine condition, steady-state test sequence on the test bed, comprising 13 modes or conditions of load and speed.

These regulations became effective in this year at levels that might be described as moderately easy for current engines, but will be tightened to very severe levels in 1975. The US Federal authorities, through the Environmental Protection Agency (EPA), have now made proposals to adopt the CARB test methods and limits (with some minor detailed changes) for 1974, and may well choose limits similar to the 1975 CARB proposals for nationwide enforcement for 1976. In addition, there are also Federal regulations on exhaust smoke, which are almost certain to be made much more severe in 1976, although the actual levels can only be currently guessed at.

For vehicles of less than 6000 lb weight, the Federal light-duty test procedures and limits apply. This is a chassis dynamometer test involving operation over a wider range of loads

34

and speeds than the CARB heavy-duty sequence. It also includes transient conditions and a cold-start sequence. Both the heavy-duty and the light-duty limits as known or guessed are summarised in Fig. 1, the guesses being indicated by the question mark after them.

a) HEAVY DUTY ENGINES

	CO g/hp h	$HC + NO_2$ g/hp h
1973 CALIFORNIA	40	16
1975 CALIFORNIA	25	5
1974 FEDERAL	40	16
1976 FEDERAL ?	25 ?	5 ?

b) PASSENGER CAR DIESEL ENGINES

	HC g/mile	CO g/mile	NO_x g/mile
PROPOSED 1975 FEDERAL	0·41	3·4	3·1
PROPOSED 1976 FEDERAL	0·41	3·4	0·4

EXHAUST OPACITY (LIGHT AND HEAVY DUTY)

1974 FEDERAL	20 % AVERAGE OBSCURATION DURING ACCELERATION. 15 % AVERAGE OBSCURATION DURING LUG MODE. 50 % PEAK.
1975/6 ?	10 % DURING LUG MODE ? 20 % PEAK?

Fig. 1   US emissions legislation

Of other countries, Japan is known to be considering urgently what limits and test procedures should be applied to automotive diesel engines, but no firm proposals have as yet become known. No other country appears at the present time to be likely to introduce such legislation in the near future.

Similarly, no other engine applications, with the exception of mines locomotives, are covered by legislation, although there is no doubt that, in the USA, off-highway vehicles, locomotive engines and other equipment will soon have some legislation applied to them.

It is also possible that other pollutants or effects may be covered by legislation in the future: possible examples are sulphur dioxide (SO_2) and exhaust odour. All diesel fuel (i.e. gas oils) contain sulphur, the natural level depending on the source of the crude. Extraction is technically feasible, and all automotive fuels contain only a relatively small amount, of about 0·2%, although complete removal would add greatly to the base cost of the fuel. However, control of SO_2 emissions within the engine does not appear to be at all possible, so that, apart from exhaust-gas scrubbing treatment, removal at source appears to be the only solution at the present time.

Diesel-exhaust odour is, of course, essentially a hydrocarbon problem, and has been of considerable concern in the USA, owing to the special circumstances there. It can be a significant problem with some types of combustion system. Introduction of legislation has up to now been delayed by the complete lack of any practical means of measuring odour quantitatively in such a way as to correlate satisfactorily with subjective assessments. This situation may however change in the near future.

3 Emissions instrumentation and measurement

For development testing and certification of engines, methods more convenient than the original chemical tests are needed for the determination of emissions concentrations, and considerable work has been carried out in this area, inevitably orientated toward the American scene. For the CARB and US Federal heavy-duty tests, the following instrumentation is used:

Carbon monoxide (CO)   :   nondispersive infrared gas analyser

Total hydrocarbons (HC):   heated (180°C) flame ionisation detector

Oxides of nitrogen (NO_x) :   nondispersive infrared gas analyser measuring nitric oxide (NO) concentrations only.

Note that, for these heavy-duty tests, the NO measurement is converted to NO_2 equivalent mathematically — in practice, the actual nitrogen-dioxide (NO_2) emissions from a diesel engine are very small indeed except perhaps at light loads.

For the light-duty procedures, the constant-volume-sampling (C.V.S.) procedure is used as for the gasoline engine, except that continuous sampling from the system into a heated flame ionisation detector is specified for HC measurement. The C.V.S. procedure requires the chemiluminescence method to be used for NO_x, which detects both NO and NO_2.

All the above methods are indirect, and continuous calibration (spanning) of the analysers is essential. Even so, the overall accuracy of the methods used is not high by absolute standards, say about ±5% in the case of CO and NO, and, in particular, the HC measurements at the low levels now being reached must be evaluated with caution since the overall accuracy here is only about ±15%. These questions are discussed in References 4 and 5. In addition to these purely instrumental problems, the question of the natural variability over a period of time of the engine performance itself must not be forgotten, and this could be of the order of ±2% on the combined HC + NO_2 emissions.

4 Basic NO_x emission characteristics — D.I. and swirl chamber engines

A typical direct-injection (D.I.) and the Ricardo Comet Mk.V swirl-chamber combustion system are illustrated in Fig. 2.

Tests on a single-cylinder 1·6 litre swept volume engine equipped with such alternative combustion systems reported by Torpey et al. (Reference 6) have already demonstrated the superior emission characteristics of the swirl chamber specially in regard to oxides of nitrogen.

The reason for the lower emissions of the swirl chamber are complex and open to debate, but major factors in determining the levels of emissions of NO_x are undoubtedly the time for the start of combustion and the mode of combustion itself. In general, swirl chambers require combustion to begin close to top dead-centre position for optimum performance, and, under these conditions, the delay period between injection and combustion is short. Therefore there is little uncontrolled burning within the chamber in the head, and the heat release proceeds smoothly but rapidly relatively late in the cycle. By the time combustion is taking place in the space outside of the head and within the piston cavities, the piston is already beginning to descend. Conditions are therefore changing rapidly towards temperatures that will be too low for the formation of significant quantities of NO.

36

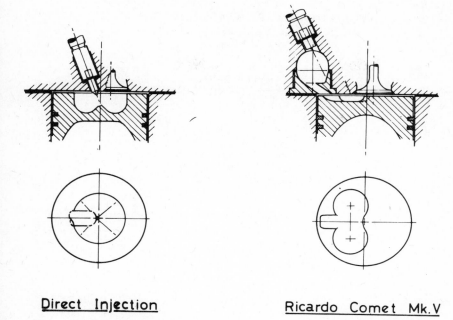

Direct Injection   Ricardo Comet Mk.V

Fig. 2   Diesel combustion systems

Combustion in the direct-injection engine of classic four spray bowl-in-piston form
proceeds on different lines, and, to obtain the optimum smokefree performance,
a start of combustion some 5-7 crank degrees ahead of the inner dead-centre position
is required. In addition, the injection-delay period is relatively long, with an
appreciable quantity of vaporised fuel present in the chamber at the moment of
ignition. Combustion of this fuel is therefore very rapid leading to high local flame
temperature, and, with the combustion air concentrated close to these advancing
flame fronts, conditions are ideal for the formation of NO.

Retarding the injection timing on the D.I. engine to give a start of combustion in the
same order as that of the swirl chamber depreciates the smoke-limited performance
and reduces the emissions of NO, but these are still appreciably higher. It is not
until the timing of the D.I. is retarded to give a start of combustion between 5 and
10° late that the emissions of NO are comparable with those of the swirl chamber.
The essential differences of the two systems can perhaps be best summarised by the
curves shown in Fig. 3, which provides average data on the emission of NO and
performance characteristics of naturally aspirated multicylinder swirl-chamber and
direct-injection engines when operating at the same air/fuel ratio of 21:1. The
general shapes of the NO curves for the two systems are similar, but the important
differences in the shapes of the smoke curves should be noted, since it is this that
allows the swirl chamber to be operated in a retarded, low-emissions mode with little
derate. Reference 7 discusses the reasons for this.

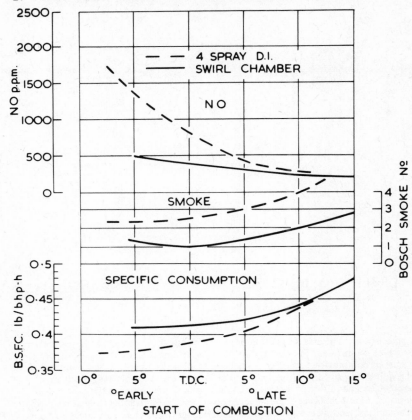

Fig. 3   NO emission and performance characteristics of D.I. and swirl chambers

5   The swirl-chamber engine

(a)   Naturally aspirated

Tests reported by Torpey et al. (Reference 6) on the single-cylinder swirl-chamber engine referred to above have now been supplemented by tests on multicylinder units, some of which are in current production in Europe and others have been converted to swirl chambers from existing direction-injection units. Very good emission levels have been observed on all these units, which range in individual cylinder size from 500 c^3 to 5 l with 4 − 12 cylinders.

In general, it has been found that, with the injection equipment set for optimum performance as judged by the minimum specific fuel consumption, the combined emissions of HC + NO$_2$ determined over the CARB 13-mode-cycle conditions lie between 5 and 8 g/bhp-h. These differences are very largely due to the individual manufacturers' choice of injection equipment and settings.

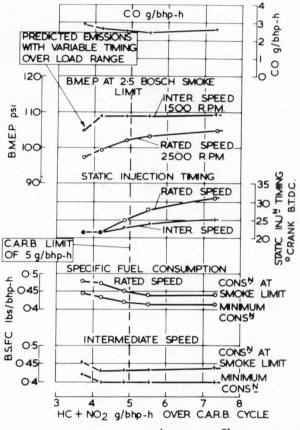

CO g/bhp-h

PREDICTED EMISSIONS
WITH VARIABLE TIMING
OVER LOAD RANGE

B.M.E.P AT 2·5 BOSCH SMOKE
LIMIT

INTER. SPEED
1500 R.P.M.

RATED SPEED
2500 R.P.M.

STATIC INJECTION TIMING

RATED SPEED

INTER. SPEED

C.A.R.B. LIMIT
OF 5 g/bhp-h

SPECIFIC FUEL CONSUMPTION

RATED SPEED   CONS^N AT
                     SMOKE LIMIT
                     MINIMUM
                     CONS^N

INTERMEDIATE SPEED

                     CONS^N AT
                     SMOKE LIMIT
                     MINIMUM
                     CONS^N

HC + NO$_2$ g/bhp-h OVER C.A.R.B. CYCLE

6 CYLINDER 416 cu in $(6800\ cm^3)$ NATURALLY
ASPIRATED SWIRL CHAMBER ENGINE

Fig. 4   Effect of injection timing on emissions over C.A.R.B. 13-mode cycle

The importance of injection timing, and hence the start of combustion on the emission of NO_x, has already been mentioned, and, in any investigation of the emission characteristics of a given engine, it is always the first factor to be examined. By careful assessment of performance, smoke and emissions, it is possible to establish those injection timings that will provide any predetermined level of emissions together with the performance that can be achieved for those emissions. Some typical results of one such investigation carried out on a naturally aspirated 6-cylinder engine of total swept volume of 6·8 l is shown in Fig. 4. These show that, with the production injection timing, the combined emissions of the engine over the CARB cycle are 7·3 g/bhp-h. The elimination of the speed advance device to operate with a fixed static-injection timing for all speeds reduces the combined emissions to 4·2 g/bhp-h. The influence of these changes in timing on the performance is also illustrated in Fig. 4, from which it will be seen that the emission of 4·2 g/bhp-h can be achieved without sacrifice of performance at the intermediate speed and at a penalty of some 5% loss in power at the rated speed. It may be considered that a condition that provides an emission of 4·2 g/bhp-h is adequate to meet the 5 g/bhp-h target, but, if even lower emissions are required, they can be realised by the adoption of variable injection timing over the load as well as the speed range. These variable timing characteristics over the load range are required to ensure that the emissions of HC when operating at light load are not excessive, and an advanced timing is therefore required at this condition; however, to lower the emissions of NO in the mid load range, a more retarded timing is then required. This retarded timing can also be employed up to full load, although, insome instances, there is value in effecting a further small advance of timing towards full load, to increase the power at some expense of NO. Use of a load-sensitive timing control does not appear to be justified, unless emission levels below 4·2 g/bhp-h for a naturally aspirated swirl-chamber unit are required.

(b) Turbocharged

The response of the swirl-chamber combustion system to turbocharging has been established on a variety of engines, and all have shown the same favourable trend. Fortnagel (Reference 8) also reports in a similar vein.

The most comprehensive tests have been made on the same 6·8 l engine used for the tests reported in Section 4. No change was made to the engine build, and the compression ratio therefore remained at 20:1. A summary of the results of an injection-timing investigation is shown in Fig. 5. For these tests, arbitrary limits to the power settings at the rated and intermediate speeds were imposed to simulate an appropriate torque curve for automotive application. The brake mean effective pressure at the rated speed of 2500 rev/min was fixed at 140 psi (lb/in^2) and at the intermediate speed of 1500 rev/min, the brake mean effective pressure was set at 155 psi. The exhaust condition was at all times below 2·5 Bosch, which is approximately equal to 5% opacity for an engine of this size.

Fig. 5 reveals that combined emissions of HC + NO_2 down to 4·2 g/bhp-h can be achieved by the use of the appropriate injection timing. This level of emissions can be achieved without derating in so far as power or torque is concerned, but the increase in fuel consumption amounts to some 6% above the value recorded with the injection timing set to give optimum specific consumption.

The possible gain in emissions offered by the adoption of a flexible pump-timing characteristic over the load range, as shown on the curves in Fig. 5, is rather less than that quoted for the normally aspirated condition, and, if required, it would permit a reduction in the combined emissions to approximately 4 g/bhp-h. The specified fuel consumption at the intermediate speed could also be lowered by this means.

Turbocharging has also reduced the specific emission of CO by some 20%.

(c)   Turbocharged and aftercooled

Tests have been made to establish the influence of turbocharging in conjunction with aftercooling on the swirl-chamber engine. As before, the work was carried out on the 6-cylinder unit, and the aftercooling was achieved by means of a water-to-air heat exchanger, with the cooling water provided by the main supply. Two degrees of aftercooling were evaluated, one test being made with the intake temperature limited to 90°C, and the second at 45°C, although the capacity of the heat exchanger was such that the latter temperature could not be held at the 100% load rated speed condition. For this single point, the air temperature in the inlet manifold rose to 75°. The results are summarised in Table 1.

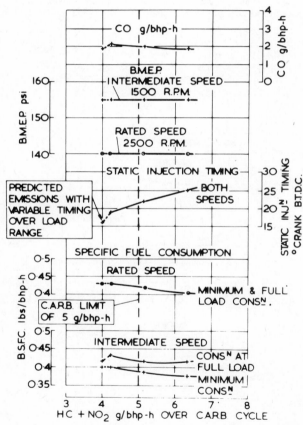

6 CYLINDER 416 cu in (6800 cm^3) TURBO-CHARGED
SWIRL CHAMBER ENGINE

Fig. 5   Effect of injection timing on emissions over C.A.R.B. 13-mode cycle

These tests were all carried out at the injection timings selected to give the best emissions under non-after-cooled conditions. Analysis of the results of additional tests made over a range of injection timings under the after-cooled conditions ijndicated that, by a reselection of injection timing, combined emissions as low as 3·2 g/bhp-h could be obtained with the 45°C intake temperature condition.

This degree of aftercooling is really only possible under marine conditions, and the results with aftercooling to 90°C are of more interest for automotive applications. The performance achieved over the load range when operating at an injection setting giving combined emissions in the order of 3·6 g/bhp-h is shown in Figure 6. There are two points that should be borne in mind when considering the levels of fuel consumption shown on these curves. The first is that the engine is not large in total swept volume, and one would expect a larger engine operating over a narrower speed range to return a better brake specific consumption, because the mechanical efficiency and heat loss to coolant will be more favourable with the larger cylinder. Secondly, the level of emission at 3·6 g/bhp-h is perhaps unnecessarily low, and, if the injection timings are set slightly more advanced to give, say, a combined emission of 4·2 g/bhp-h, the specific fuel consumption would be improved to the values shown on the curves.

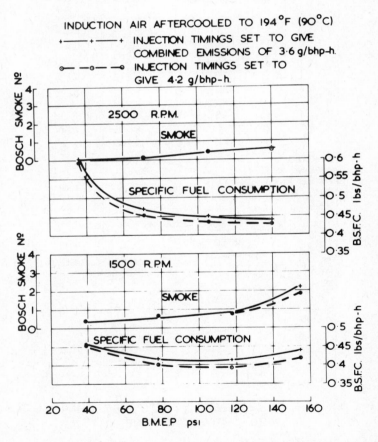

Fig. 6   Performance curves at different emission levels

(d) Timing of events and maximum cylinder pressures

The steps taken to reduce the emissions of the swirl-chamber engine have also provided a bonus in the form of a reduction of the combustion noise. With injection commencing 4 or 5 crank degrees ahead of top dead centre, it is often difficult to detect the precise time for the start of combustion because of the smooth diagram. Almost invariably, the compression pressure is the maximum cylinder pressure, and the pressure rise due to the start of combustion around $5 - 8^{\circ}$ late merely results in a swelling of the expansion diagram. The compression pressures, however, may be relatively high, as, for example, when operating under the turbocharged non-after-cooled condition, values in the order of 1650 psi were recorded at 2500 rev/min full load.

(e) Heat loss to coolant

The characteristics of a swirl-chamber combustion system, of very high gas velocities within the chamber, are beneficial to mixing and performance under low-emissions conditions but do give rise to high local heat flows and gross heat-rejection rates. Test work has shown that gross heat-rejection rates are not increased by operation in the retarded low-emissions mode, but it is clear that a change from D.I. to swirl-chamber system, to obtain low emissions, will require a coolant radiator of some 30–50% increase in capacity to be fitted.

(f) Exhaust-gas recirculation

This is by now an accepted method of reducing the emissions of oxides of nitrogen of gasoline engines, and its value in reducing the peak cycle temperatures as well as displacing oxygen to limit the quantity available for the oxidation of nitrogen is equally applicable to the diesel engine.

The emission characteristics of the normally aspirated swirl-chamber engine are particularly suited to gas recirculation, because, if variable dilution over the load range is employed, the peak emission of NO that occurs below full load can be lowered without affecting the full-load performance in any way. The engine will, however, be operating nearer to its smoke limit over a greater part of the load and speed range. This will be clear from the curves shown in Fig. 7, which illustrates the influence of exhaust-gas recirculation on the performance of a multi-cylinder engine over the load range at 1700 rev/min.

In these tests, the exhaust gas was cooled to a temperature of 50°C before reaspiration, and this could be regarded as being an impractical value, but it was chosen to demonstrate the maximum benefit in regard to the emission of NO. It will be seen that there is a marked drop in the smoke-limited performance, as the quantity of re-cycled gas is increased, although the onset of smoke occurs long before there is any significant change of fuel consumption.

The influence of recirculation on the CARB emissions of this engine is shown in Table 2. It should be noted that the injection timings selected for these tests were those required for optimum performance.

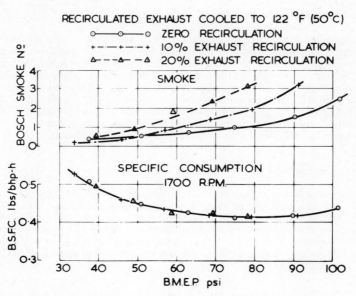

Fig. 7   Effect of exhaust-gas recirculation on performance and smoke of 6-cylinder swirl-chamber engine over load range at 1700 r.p.m.

Table 1

Effect of aftercooling on emissions: turbocharged 6-cylinder 416 in^3 swirl-chamber engine

Condition	Emissions over CARB cycle, g/bhp-h			
	CO	HC	NO_2	$HC + NO_2$
No charge cooling, inlet temperature 266°F (130°C) at 100% load rated speed	2·2	0·7	3·5	4·2
Aftercooled to inlet temperature of 194°F (90°C) at 100% load rated speed	1·9	0·7	2·9	3·6
Aftercooled to inlet temperature of 113°F (45°C), except at 100% load rated speed, when temperature was 167°F (75°C)	1·7	0·7	2·8	3·5

Table 2

Effect of exhaust-gas recirculation on emission levels from a 480 in^3 Comet V engine

Condition	Emissions over CARB cycle, g/bhp-h			
	CO	HC	NO$_2$	HC + NO$_2$
No exhaust recirculation	3·6	0·8	7·1	7·9
Variable recirculation of exhaust gas cooled to 122°F (50°C)	2·4	0·7	5·3	6·0

This appreciable reduction in combined emission was achieved by the use of variable recirculation employing 20% up to 50% load, 10% at 75% load and no recirculation at full load. However, exhaust-gas recirculation alone is not sufficient to lower the emission levels of a swirl-chamber engine tuned for maximum performance to be within the 5 g/bhp-h target, and it would therefore have to be employed in conjunction with timing retard to meet these levels.

It has already been demonstrated that the required emission levels can be met by the simple means of retardation of timing, and therefore the complication of exhaust-gas recirculation does not appear to be justified to meet the present emission levels. If these limits are lowered still further in the future, there may be merit in its use. At the same time, the increase in complexity, and hence first cost, and the possible adverse effects of exhaust-gas recirculation engine durability would have to be considered.

(g)   Influence of spray position and form on the emissions of HC

Test work has shown that varying the angle, and hence radial position, of the fuel spray within the swirl chamber has a significant influence on the HC emission levels. However, it was found that, for a nozzle and hence spray form of given type, the emissions were at a minimum in the position selected in the past on grounds of performance alone.

These tests also showed that nozzle type could have a large effect on HC emission levels at the same nominal spray position. Unlike the D.I. engine discussed later, these changes did not correlate with the volume in the nozzle, downstream of the needle seat, in which fuel could be trapped. It is therefore clear that spray characteristics, including no doubt, the relative penetration and the degree and distribution of atomisation, are of relevance in this type of chamber. Work is in hand to obtain a better understanding of these problems, but it is already very clear that characteristics must be such as to give a sharp cutoff to the injection, with no dribble or late secondary injections.

6   The direct-injection engine

The majority of automotive diesel engines installed in vehicles having a gross weight exceeding 6000 lb, and therefore subject to the US Federal or Californian regulations, employ some form of direct-injection combustion system. The investment in the tooling to produce these engines, coupled with their good fuel consumption, low heat loss to coolant and general freedom from problems of thermal loading, ensures that manufacturers will be reluctant to abandon their current practice without good reason. The question therefore is, can the direct-injection engine be developed to meet the legislative requirements while retaining its lead in regard to specific performance and first cost?

(a) Naturally aspirated

The curves in Fig. 8 illustrate the results of a timing investigation made on a direct-injection engine of European design having a total swept volume of approximately 5·9 l. Fig. 8 shows that, at the manufacturer's current production injection timing of 23°E, the combined emissions over the CARB cycle are just within the 1973 requirement of 16 g/bhp-h. Therefore it is typical of most naturally aspirated engines employing open-chamber combustion systems in conjunction with inlet-port-induced swirl and four spray nozzles. Progressive retardation of the injection timing results in a notable reduction in the combined emissions, although this is accompanied by a serious loss of smoke-limited performance.

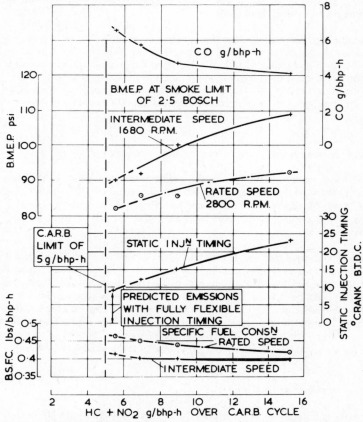

Fig. 8   Effect of injection timing on combined emissions of 6-cylinder 360 in^3 (5900 cm^3) naturally aspirated direct-injection engine

46

The lowest emission that can be achieved by timing retard alone is 6·9 g/bhp-h — any further retard of timing beyond the setting giving this figure results in a rise in the combined emission. This is because the reduction in NO due to timing retard is more than offset by the increase in HC as the combustion deteriorates and the misfire condition is approached. The increase in emission of CO at the retarded timing will also be noted.

The adoption of a fully flexible injection characteristic providing variable timing over the load range would permit the emissions of HC at light load to be held in check, and by this additional complication to the injection equipment, the combined emissions could be reduced to approximately 5·5 g/bhp-h.

This particular engine was fitted with nozzles having a sac volume below the needle seat of approximately 1·5mm³. In the light of experience on other engines at Shoreham, and as reported elsewhere (Reference 9) it is certain that further reduction in the emission of HC could be realised by the use of nozzles having a reduced sac volume below the seat. The value of these nozzles in achieving this end is illustrated in Fig. 9, which shows the results of tests made on a single-cylinder 1·6 litre engine with nozzles having sac volumes of 1·3 mm³ and 0·5 mm³.

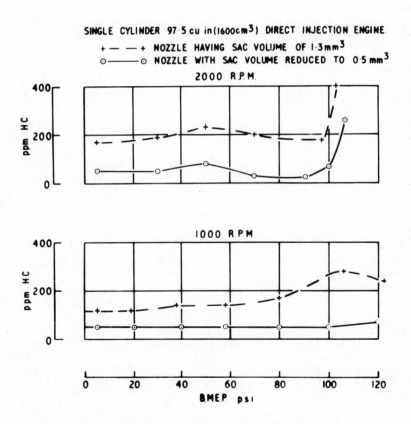

Fig. 9   Effect of nozzle sac volume on emissions of HC

The gain in the CARB emission of HC if nozzles of this type were adopted for the multicylinder engine referred to in Figs. 12 and 13 could amount to as much as 1·0 g/bhp-h, bringing the combined emissions down to 4·5 g/bhp-h, assuming that the flexible timing pump was also employed. Although this figures is below the legislative requirement, there is little in reserve; moreover, the performance achieved at these emission levels represents a 20% derate on the current production performance. Therefore, to meet a given power requirement, a naturally aspirated D.I. engine would have to be increased in swept volume, and a larger, heavier and more expensive engine would result.

Tests made on other naturally aspirated D.I. engines of both larger and smaller cylinder sizes have confirmed this general trend. Therefore there seems little prospect of the naturally aspirated D.I. engine being a viable proposition, unless combustion and/or injection systems can be developed that will overcome the principal defects: (i) the serious decline in smoke-limited performance that accompanies the retardation of timing required to lower the emission of NO, and (ii) the relatively high emissions of HC. With regard to (i), tests at Shoreham have shown that increase of cylinder swirl level as sometimes advocated does not improve the specific emissions, if already correctly matched for optimum performance. Similarly, increases in injection rate obtained with conventional injection equipment do not reduce the specific emissions even if the smoke-limited performance may improve slightly.

If the object is to lower the emissions of NO while maintaining a clean exhaust at a good level of performance, as well as keeping the emission of HC and CO within bounds, what alternative solutions are available?

The possibilities are:

(i)   to operate at retarded timings in the interests of low emissions and to attempt to clean up the smoke by turbocharging and aftercooling.

(ii)   to reduce the emissions by means of exhaust-gas recirculation or water injection

(iii)   to attempt to modify the heat-release diagram of the open chamber to inhibit the formation of oxides of nitrogen during the initial uncontrolled rate of burning. This could be achieved by means of pilot injection, fumigation, or other changes to the injection characteristics and combustion-chamber configuration that will reduce the combustion delay period.

(iv)   the possible use of catalysts to control the emissions of HC and CO.

Most of these solutions are being studied by the author's company, and, although it is not possible to present results from some of the projects at the present time, some general observations can be made.

(b) Turbocharged

The results of tests made on a turbocharged direct-injection engine of approximately 11 000 cm^3 total swept volume are shown in Fig. 10. It will be seen that the predicted emissions for the engine, assuming that fully flexible injection timings are employed, are just below 5 g/bhp-h, but the loss in smoke-limited power at the intermediate speed is such as to bring the torque available at this speed to the same level as that achieved at the rated speed. Derating of the engine at full speed to provide a torque rise results in slightly higher combined emissions, because, with this particular engine, the brake specific emissions of NO at the rated speed are rising slightly with reduction of load. The depreciation of specific fuel consumption necessary to achieve the low

48

emission levels will be noted, and reference to Fig. 5 shows that the swirl-chamber engine operating under similar non-aftercooled turbocharged conditions has been returning specific fuel consumptions of the same order as the D.I., without the necessity of derating.

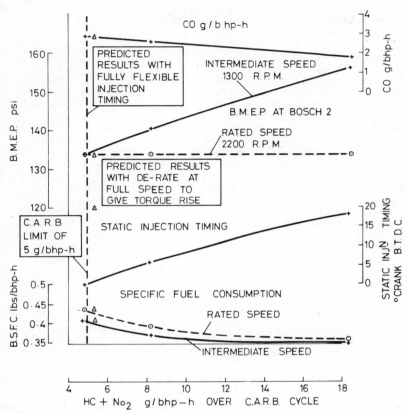

Fig. 10 Effect of injection timing on combined emissions of turbocharged 685 in³ (11100 cm³) direct-injection engine

Other tests made on a turbocharged 6-cylinder direct-injection engine of a rather smaller volume of 4·9 litres has returned combinations of rather higher levels, but the response to derating is more favourable (Table 3).

Table 3

Effect of turbocharge on emissions: 6-cylinder 300 in³ direct-injection engine

Condition	Predicted emissions of HC + NO$_2$ with fully flexible timing g/bhp-h
Turbocharged at naturally aspirated rating	6·6
Turbocharged to 33% above naturally aspirated rating	7·0

49

As can be seen, the lowest levels of emissions reached on the 4·9 litre engine are rather higher than those shown for the larger engine, but relatively little work has been done to optimise the matching of the injection equipment and the turbocharger on this smaller unit. Nevertheless, there are several other factors apart from cylinder size, such as differences in combustion-chamber design and in swirl, as well as the number of injector spray holes, which are also relevant and which could all be playing their part in determining the absolute emission levels.

(c) Turbocharged and aftercooled

The value of an aftercooler in reducing the emissions of the turbocharged swirl-chamber engine has already been noted, and similar gains are to be expected with the direct-injection engine according to the degree of aftercooling adopted. With one direct-injection engine, lowering the inlet temperature from 140° to 60°C reduced the specific emissions of NO_2 from 4 to 2·9 g/bhp-h, i.e. a reduction of 1·1 g/bhp-h. This degree of aftercooling is possible with an air-to-air cooler in a moderate climate, but a more realistic aftercooling temperature would be nearer to 90°C. The gain in specific emissions at this temperature amounts to 0·6 g/bhp-h, so that the combined emissions of the 11·1 litre direct-injection engine, referred to in Section 5, operating with turbocharging and aftercooling, together with a fully flexible injection-pump timing characteristic, could be predicted at about 4·4 g/bhp-h. The performance level at these emissions will be smoke-limited at the peak torque speed to some 13% lower than is possible without emission control, and a reduction in power at the rated speed will have to be accepted if any torque rise is required. The specific fuel consumption would be comparable with those of the swirl-chamber engine shown in Fig. 6 if both engines were operating at the same rating of 120 psi at the maximum speed and 134 psi bmep at the peak torque speed.

(d) Exhaust-gas recirculation

Tests to determine the influence of exhaust-gas recirculation on the emissions of a direct-injection engine have been made for a 6-cylinder engine of approximately 14·0 l swept volume. These particular tests were aimed at establishing the reduction in emissions that could be achieved while retaining the injection settings giving the optimum performance. The results are summarised in Table 4.

Table 4

Effect of exhaust-gas recycle on emissions and smoke-limited power: naturally aspirated 6-cylinder 855 in^3 direct-injection engine

Condition	Emissions over CARB 13-mode cycle, g/bhp-h				Power loss
	CO	HC	NO_2	HC + NO_2	%
No recirculation	3·5	0·5	15·5	16	—
10% recirculation Cooled to 176°F (80°C)	5·0	0·7	9·1	9·8	13%
10% recirculation Cooled to 86°F (30°C)	4·3	0·7	9·0	9·7	10%

The loss of performance is large in spite of the fact that the quantity of exhaust gas recirculated was modest, and this had been cooled to the relatively low temperature of 80°C. The additional test, with the recycled gas to an impractically low temperature of 30°C, was made to discover if even lower emissions could be expected, but no significant improvements resulted.

The combination of exhaust-gas recirculation and timing retard has not been assessed, but no doubt, it does offer the prospect of reaching the required emission levels provided that engine durability is not adversely affected. However, these doubts, together with the complication of control and the possible need for cooling the exhaust gas before reaspiration, make it an unattractive solution.

(e)   Water injection

The value of water injection into the cylinder or by aspiration at the inlet manifold in reducing the formation of NO by lowering the cycle temperature has been demonstrated by several people working in this field (References 10 and 11). Work by the author's company on multicylinder engines has been confined to tests made with continuous injection of water into the entry of each inlet port. One set of tests was conducted with the engine tuned to give optimum performance, so that the base-line emissions were relatively high. The results are summarised in Table 5.

Table 5

Effect of continuous water injection into the intake manifold on emissions and power: naturally aspirated direct-injection engine

Condition	Emissions over CARB cycle g/bhp-h				Power loss
No water injection	CO	HC	NO_2	$HC + NO_2$	
No water injection	3·5	0·5	15·5	16	–
0·5/1 water/fuel	4·3	0·5	11·4	11·9	2%
1/1 water/fuel	4·7	0·6	7·8	8·4	4%
0·5/1 above 50% load	4·3	0·5	11·2	11·7	2%
1/1 above 50% load	4·7	0·6	8·0	8·6	4%

As will be seen, the loss in smoke-limited performance is very small for a marked reduction in the emissions of NO, and it is sufficient to restrict the injection of water to 50% load and above. If used in conjunction with a degree of timing retard, there are prospects that the use of water injection can provide emission levels within the target requirement of 5 g/bhp-h with the least depreciation in smoke-limited performance of any other solution, but, as with exhaust-gas recirculation, there are doubts about long-term engine durability. In addition, the provision of additional tankage resulting in loss of payload, as well as the problem of freezing of the water, further reduces its attractions.

(f)   Pilot injection

Experiments to establish the influence of the pilot injection on emissions are being pursued on a single-cylinder 1·6 litre research engine equipped with a dual-pump injection system.

The pilot and main pumps feed a common injector via pipes incorporating a nonreturn valve in the pilot line. This permits the pilot fuel to be varied both in time and in quantity relative to the main charge.

The experiments are at an early stage, but the initial results indicate that some reductions in the emissions of NO can be achieved by the selection of the appropriate pilot quantity and its phasing relative to the main injection. It would be premature at the present stage of this test programme to draw any conclusions about the prospect of pilot injection being a viable practical solution to reaching the 5 g/bhp-h target for the direct-injection engine. Considerable additional research is required, but one thing is clear: it will demand the development of new injection systems to provide the required quantity and phasing of the pilot, both of which will probably need to be varied over the load and speed range for optimum results. Piezoelectric of electromagnetic systems would seem to be most suitable to meet these requirements.

7   The diesel-engined light-duty vehicle

Passenger cars and light trucks equipped with high-speed swirl-chamber diesel engines ranging in swept volume from 1·3 to 2·2 litres have been in production in Europe for many years, finding widespread acceptance in both taxi and private-car use because of the very considerable gain in fuel economy that can be achieved compared with the equivalent gasoline-powered engine (Reference 12). The increasing need to conserve the world's fuel supplies, as well as the pressure to reduce overall emissions, therefore warrants consideration of the diesel engine as the power unit for passenger cars, light delivery vans and trucks in the USA.

Tests which Ricardo has made to establish the emission levels on current-production European-size saloon cars fitted with diesel engines have given values of the following order when tested according to the 1972 C.V.S. procedure:

HC   1·0 g/mile   CO   3·9 g/mile NO_x 1·3 g/mile

Test-bed work carried out on these same engines indicates that, if the injection characteristics were optimised for emissions, NO_x could be reduced to approximately 0·7 g/mile, leaving the emissions of HC and CO unchanged.

The cars used for these tests weighed approximately 2800 lb, fitted with engines developing 60-65 hp, and difficulties were experienced in maintaining the exact schedule of the cycle, owing to the relatively low power of the engine. If an engine of 105 hp were fitted to an American-size car weighing 4500 lb to provide the same power/weight ratio as these European cars, the gross-emissions/mile would be expected to increase in proportion to the weight of the vehicle, and they would therefore rise to:

HC   1·6 g/mile   CO   6·3 g/mile NO_x 1·1 g/mile

The performance of the vehicle with only 105 hp would probably not be acceptable in the USA, and an engine of 150 hp would be more suitable. If the power/weight ratio of the European vehicle is only assumed to be just sufficient to drive the test cycle, the vehicle having the larger engine will be driven at the same power output over the cycle but at a lower load factor. This is an important point, because, with indirect-injection engines, the specific emissions of NO_x and HC, in g/bhp-h, increase as the load is reduced, and, in consequence, the larger engines will give higher mass emissions per mile for the same output than the smaller unit. It should also be noted that the spark-ignition engine tends to behave in the opposite manner.

If the 105 hp engine is replaced by one developing 150 hp to give a more favourable power/weight ratio, test-bed data indicate that the emission of NO_x will be increased by some 25% and that of HC by 40%. The CO would remain unchanged. The final predicted emissions for a 150 hp normally aspirated diesel-engined car weighing 4500 lb (2050 kg) would therefore be:

HC   2·3 g/mile   CO   6·3 g/mile NO_x 1·4 g/mile

and these values should be compared with the 1976 Federal limits given earlier.

It is clear that further work will be required to reduce the emissions to bring the high-powered diesel car within the Federal legislation. The use of turbocharging in conjunction with exhaust-gas recirculation is a possible solution, and calculations suggest that, by these measures, the emissions of NO_x could be reduced to around 0·7 g/mile. An alternative would be to reduce the size and weight of the American car, as this would lower the specific emissions albeit at some cost in potential performance. These are penalties that may well have to be faced, because the diesel engine still offers the best all-round compromise for the conservation of fuel and high standards of emissions.

8   Summary and conclusions

The conclusions to be drawn are as follows:-

(a)   Swirl-chamber combustion system engine

(i)   The Californian 1975 regulations can be met with adequate reserves with the current-production engines having modified injection timing characteristics over the speed range.

(ii)   There is no sacrifice of performance on turbocharged engines, and only a minimal derate on the normally aspirated unit. Specific fuel consumption levels are at least as good as, or better than, those of a direct-injection engine of comparable size operating in the low-emission mode.

(iii) The swirl-chamber engine has the potential to operate with combined emissions of less than 3 g/bhp-h, provided the appropriate injection and nozzle conditions are adopted.

(iv)   Variable exhaust-gas recirculation over the load range offers potential further reductions in emissions at some additional complication and with an unknown possible adverse effect on engine durability. There is no need to adopt exhaust-gas recirculation to meet the future CARB 1975 legislation with swirl-chamber engines.

(v)   The heat loss to coolant of the swirl-chamber engine is unaffected by the changes made to achieve low emissions, but, in absolute terms, the coolant losses are high, and necessitate a large radiator.

(b)   Direct-injection engine

(i)   Subject to the use of an injection pump having variable timing characteristics over the load range, as well as the use of nozzles having low sac volumes, combined emissions just within the 5 g/bhp-h have been predicted for one normally aspirated unit.

(ii) The loss of smoke-limited performance to achieve low emissions is serious, and amounts to a 20% derate on the naturally aspirated optimum performance. Specific fuel consumptions are of the same order as those of the swirl chamber at the intermediate speeds and higher at rated speeds.

(iii) Combined emissions just within the 5 g/bhp-h target are predicted for one turbocharged direct-injection engine, but the specific fuel consumption is higher than for a swirl-chamber unit operating at the same combined emissions levels.

(iv) Turbocharged and aftercooled direct-injection engines are predicted to achieve emissions in the order of 4·5 g/bhp-h at a performance level that will be less than is possible with a swirl-chamber engine of the same size at the same level of emissions.

(v) Exhaust-gas recirculation in conjunction with timing retard offers prospects of reaching the required emission levels on direct-injection engines.

(vi) Water injection at the rate equivalent to the fuel consumption, together with a degree of timing retard, should permit the target CARB 1975 emission levels to be reached with the minimum loss of performance.

(vii) Pilot injection shows some promise in reducing emissions of NO, but may be accompanied by an increase in emissions of HC and smoke.

(c) High-speed swirl-chamber diesel engine

The passenger car or light truck powered by the high-speed swirl-chamber diesel engine could offer a compromise solution to the problems of conservation of fuel and lowering of emissions.

9 Acknowledgements

This paper has been based largely on a previous paper by one of the authors (Reference 13), which gives more information on the work by the authors' company briefly reported here. The authors wish to thank colleagues who have contributed to the work described, and, in particular, R.G. Freese, who analysed much of the data presented.

10 References

1   MARSHALL, W.F., and HURN, R.W.   'Factors influencing diesel emissions'. Paper 680528, presented at West Coast meeting, San Francisco, August 1968.

2   MARSHALL, W.F. and FLEMING, R.D.   'Diesel emissions as related to engine variables and fuel characteristics'. Paper 710836, presented at the SAE, fuels and lubricants meeting, St. Louis, October, 1971.

3   BASCOM, R.C., BROERING, L.C. and WULFHORST, D.E.   .'Design factors that affect diesel emissions'. Paper 710484, SAE SP 365, Engineering know-how engine design, p.19.

4   WAGNER, T.O. and JOHNSON, J.H.   'Co-operative evaluation of techniques for measuring hydrocarbons in diesel exhaust'. Paper 710218, presented at the SAE automotive-engineering congress, Detroit, January 1971.

5   PERCY, J.M. BROERING, L.C.,   'Co-operative evaluation of techniques for measuring
       and JOHNSON, J.H.   nitric oxide and carbon monoxide'. Paper 720104,
                                          presented at the SAE automotive-engineering congress,
                                          Detroit, January 1972.

6   TORPEY, P.M., WHITEHEAD, M.J.   'Experiments in the control of diesel emissions'.
       and WRIGHT, M.   Paper C 124/7, presented at the IMechE conference
                                          on air pollution in transport engines, Solihull,
                                          November 1971.

7   BROOME, D. and KHAN, I.M.   'The mechanisms of soot release from combustion of
                                          hydrocarbon fuels with particular reference to the
                                          diesel engine'. Paper C 140/71, presented at the
                                          IMechE converence on air pollution in transport
                                          engines, Solihull, November 1971.

8   FORTNAGEL, M.   'Influencing exhaust gas composition by means of
                                          exhaust gas recirculation in a pressure charged swirl
                                          chamber diesel engine (Presented at the University of
                                          Trier Kaiserslantern symposium on technical and
                                          legal problems of the protection of the environment,
                                          September 1971), MTZ, February 1972.

9   HAMES, R.J., MERRION, D.F.   'Some effects of fuel injection system parameters
       and FORD, H.S.   on diesel exhaust emissions'. Paper 710671,
                                          SAE national West Coast meeting, Vancouver, BC,
                                          August 1971.

10 VALDMANIS, E., and   'The effects of emulsified fuels and water injection
       WULFHORST, D.E.   on diesel combustion'. Paper 700736 presented at
                                          the SAE industrial machinery and powerplant
                                          meeting, Milwaukie, September 1970.

11 ABTHOFF, J.,   'Measurement and variation of the emissions of
                                          oxides of nitrogen from internal combustion engines
                                          by measures applied to the engine and by ancillary
                                          devices' (Combustion Engines Research Association,
                                          Frankfurt on Main, 1968).

12 WALDER, C.J.   'Some problems encountered in the design and
                                          development of high speed diesel engines'. Paper
                                          978A, presented at the SAE international automotive-
                                          engineering congress, detroit, January 1965.

13 WALDER, C.J.   'Reduction of emissions from diesel engines'. Paper
                                          730214, presented at SAE international automotive-
                                          engineering congress, Detroit, January 1973.

5 The differential compound engine

Prof. F.J. Wallace, D.Sc., Ph.D., C.Eng., F.I.Mech.E.
School of Engineering, Bath University of Technology, England.
and
K. Sivakumaran

1 Introduction

One of the authors has been concerned over some 12 years with the development of the general concept of the differential compound engine (DCE), which, initially, was regarded as a means of achieving the following primary objectives, all particularly relevant in the context of traction prime movers:

(a)   high unit output by the use of high supercharge pressures

(b)   high torque backup with reduction in output-shaft speed as a means
of eliminating, or greatly simplifying, conventional transmission systems.

These aspects have been reported in a number of papers (References 1–4), and it may fairly be claimed that the experimental unit now running in the University of Bath, initially equipped with a 2-stroke opposed-piston diesel engine, but now employing a more conventional 6-cylinder 4-stroke diesel engine, has substantially realised these expectations.

In the most recent paper on the DCE (Reference 5), certain additional aspects have been commented on, particularly

(a)   fuel economy

(b)   dynamic response

(c)   emission and noise levels

It is particularly appropriate that these latter aspects should be dealt with in some detail. It may justifiably be claimed that the DCE, in its present form, with very flexible multivariable engine-operating control (fuel input, airflow by bypass valve, boost level by variable turbine-nozzle control), is indeed a low-emission engine. In addition, the present paper provides the first comprehensive set of experimental results obtained with the 4-stroke diesel engine.

2 Basic concept of DCE

The basic layout of the plant is shown in Fig. 1. The engine drives the ring gear of a fully floating epicyclic gearbox. The planet carrier is geared to the output shaft, which, in turn, receives a direct power input from the exhaust turbine connected by direct spur reduction gearing. The supercharging compressor (of the rotary positive-displacement type) is driven by the sunwheel member of the epicyclic gear train.

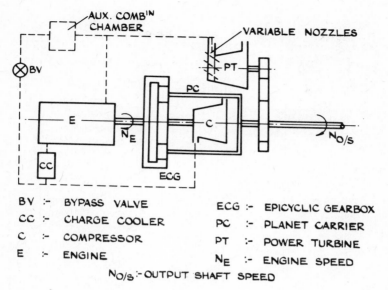

BV :- BYPASS VALVE   ECG :- EPICYCLIC GEARBOX
CC :- CHARGE COOLER   PC :- PLANET CARRIER
C :- COMPRESSOR   PT :- POWER TURBINE
E :- ENGINE N_E :- ENGINE SPEED
              $N_{O/S}$:- OUTPUT SHAFT SPEED

Fig. 1   D.C.E. layout

The speed relationships for the engine-compressor-output shaft train incorporated in the experimental rig are shown in Fig. 2, and show the well known trend of all differ-ential gear trains, namely speeding up of the compressor shaft when the output shaft is slowed down, while the engine speed is kept constant. The arrangement makes it possible for the engine to operate under optimum conditions for any given level of power demanded, irrespective of output shaft speed, and provides the basis for very high torque backup.

The gas flowpath is also indicated in Fig. 1. Air delivered by the Lysholm-type compressor divides into two flows namely:

(a)   to the engine through an aftercooler CC

(b)   direct to the turbine through a bypass line controlled by a bypass valve BV.

The engine exhaust gases combine with the bypass flow, and then pass through the single stage inward radial flow exhaust turbine which has been specially equipped with fully variable nozzles.

Control of the unit is thus through three simultaneous 'inputs', namely:

(a)   fuel-rack setting, controlling power

(b)   bypass-valve setting, controlling engine-scavenge ratio

(c)   turbine-nozzle setting, controlling boost level

which enable any load demand (i.e. combination of output shaft speed and torque) to be met so as to satisfy certain external constraints, such as optimum overall efficiency.

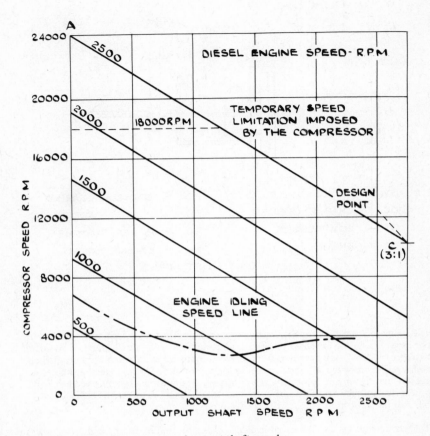

Fig. 2   Engine compressor and output shaft speeds

Typical experimental output-shaft (O/S) torque and power envelopes are shown in Figs. 3 and 4, and demonstrate both the 'constant power', and hence implied high torque backup, characteristics of the unit, and the relatively wide operating field over which reasonable overall efficiencies are achieved. In connection with the latter, it is relevant to point out that the exceptionally heavy construction of the experimental epicyclic gearbox unit has led to parasitic losses that would be well in excess of those encountered in a well designed automotive unit.

However, it is obvious that gearbox losses up to 30 hp in relation to maximum output-shaft power of 175 hp and maximum engine power of 235 hp constitutes a serious penalty.

The leading particulars of the experimental unit are given in Table 1.

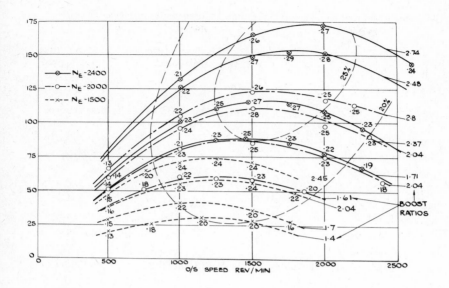

Fig. 3   Experimental power curves

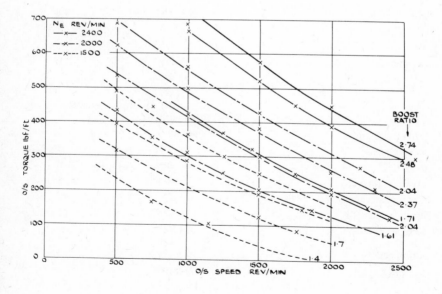

Fig. 4   Experimental torque curves

59

Table 1

Basic specification of experimental DCE unit (theoretical performance figures)

	Maximum output-shaft speed	Zero output-shaft speed
Diesel Engine		
Type	Perkins 6·354 4-stroke diesel engine, high-output version	
Swept volume	354 in^3	
Compression ratio	11·8 : 1 effective	
Crankshaft speed	2500 rev/min	
bmep, lbf/in^2	204	207
bhp	228	231
Scavenge ratio	1·03	1·03
Trapped-air/fuel ratio	32·5	32·4
Boost/pressure ratio	3·00	3·00
Maximum cycle pressure (lbf/in^2)	1500	1500
Brake thermal efficiency	0·326	0·325
Compressor		
Type	2 rotary positive displacement Godfrey SRM type 208	
Airflow (lb/min)	67·1	163·5
Speed (rev/min)	11363	24000
Pressure ratio	3·05	3·05
Efficiency	0·68	0·77
Horsepower	108	231
Turbine		
Type	Napier CO 45 inward radial flow fitted with variable nozzles	
Speed (rev/min)	50750	0
Pressure ratio	2·98	3·07
Efficiency	0·69	0
Mass flow (lb/min)	68·6	165·0
Inlet temperature (^{O}K)	1393	1049
Nozzle angle (^{O})	7·62	15·92
Horsepower	100·5	0
Output Shaft		
Speed (rev/min)	2500	0
Torque (lbf ft)	465	1065
Horsepower	220·4	0
Overall efficiency	0·315	0

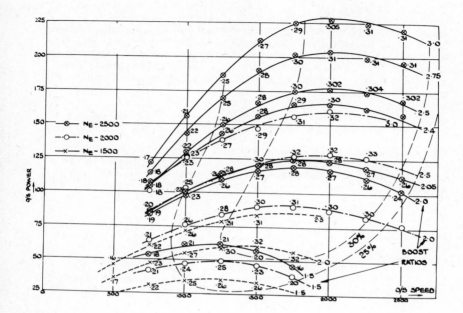

Fig. 5   Theoretical power curves

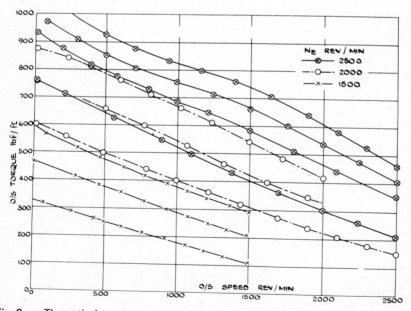

Fig. 6   Theoretical torque curves

61

The performance figures in Table 1 do not allow for gear losses whereas the performance curves for output shaft power and torque (Fig. 3 and 4) are experimentally obtained values. Figs. 5 and 6 are corresponding theoretical results, using specially developed matching programs, which have been described elsewhere (References 1 − 5). The trends in the two sets of curves are very similar, discrepancies between theoretical and achieved results being due primarily to epicyclic gearbox losses, which have been investigated separately and account for up to 30 hp at high engine and output-shaft speeds.

3   Steady state operating conditions − control system

Figs. 3 and 4, as well as Figs. 5 and 6, give a wide range of operating conditions, and indicate the salient feature of the unit, namely a very high rate of torque backup leading to a greatly simplified transmission system as well as very flexible control achievable by simultaneous adjustment of

(a)   fuel-rack setting

(b)   bypass-valve control

(c)   turbine-nozzle setting.

The experimental tests were run at three primary engine speeds, namely 2400, 2000 and 1500 rev/min, and at boost-pressure ratio settings of approximately 1·6, 2·0, 2·4 and 2·8 at each of these speeds, with the output-shaft speed varying from 500 to 2500 rev/min. The control system must be such as to choose automatically an optimum combination of turbine nozzle and bypass setting for a given power demand, i.e. a given combination of output-shaft speed and torque. By 'optimum' setting is meant a combination of settings giving best economy or best emission levels, though the latter will be discussed in a separate section.

Thus, in Figs. 5 and 6, applicable to the theoretical results, it is seen that two engine settings, namely

(a)   speed N_e = 2500 rev/min, boost-pressure ratio r_c = 2·4

(b)   speed N_e = 2000 rev/min, boost-pressure ratio r_c = 3·0

give very similar torque and power curves over the greater part of the output-shaft speed range. Similarly, N_e = 2500 rev/min, r_c = 2·05, on the one hand, and N_e = 2000 rev/min, r_c = 2·5, on the other, provide almost identical output-shaft conditions. In Table 2, the first pair of settings (a and b above) is compared at an output-shaft speed of 2000 rev/min.

Clearly, condition (b) is advantageous in terms of improved overall and engine efficiencies. With regard to emission levels, the situation is less clear cut, and the limitations of simple equilibrium calculations, on which the NO-concentration figures are based, must be borne in mind. The maximum cycle temperatures and NO concentrations are closely comparable, so that, if frozen-equilibrium considerations were to be applied, there would be a marginal gain with condition (a). In either case, however, the inherently high air/fuel ratios result in relatively low NO concentrations. This low NO characteristic of the DCE is reinforced by the low engine-exhaust and the even lower turbine-inlet temperatures (1090 and 1316 °R, respectively). It is probably safe to predict that the combination of high air/fuel ratio, low turbine-inlet temperature owing to mixing with bypass air (see Fig. 1), and long residence time in the exhaust system, is conducive to exceptionally low NO as well as CO levels, the calculated values for the latter being zero except at the maximum cycle temperature.

Table 2

Effect of varying control settings for given load demand (theoretical values)

	Setting (a)	Setting (b)
Output-shaft power	165·4	161·9
Overall efficiency	0·300	0·319
Engine power (hp)	183·5	184·2
Engine bmep (lbf/in^2)	164·1	205·9
Engine efficiency	0·332	0·363
Engine trapped-air/fuel ratio	33·9	35·4
Peak cycle pressure (lbf/in^2)	1500	1500
Peak cycle temperature ($^{\circ}$R)	3152	3208
Engine-exhaust temperature	1426	1378
Turbine-inlet temperature ($^{\circ}$R)	1090	1316
Cylinder concentration of NO (rev/min)	2721	3067
Engine-exhaust concentration of NO	1·52	0·95
Turbine-inlet concentration of NO	0·03	0·51

Hence the control setting optimisation is essentially concerned with maximising engine and overall efficiency, and here it is clear that, for a given demanded power level, a combination of lowest engine speed consistent with mechanically permissible boost levels and the availability of adequate air mass flow — which would otherwise imply a reduction in boost level — is desirable.

A tentative optimum schedule based on the theoretical performance curves of Figs. 5 and 6 is indicated in Table 3.

Table 3

Optimum operating schedule

Output-shaft power level (approx)(hp)	80	125	200
Engine power level (approx)(hp)	105	148	210
Engine boost-pressure ratio	2·5	2·5	2·75
Engine speed (rev/min)	1500	2000	2500
Engine bmep (lbf/in^2)	160	166	190
Engine trapped-air/fuel ratio	42	38	33

4 Acceleration characteristics

Only a limited programme of tests concerned with transient response of the experimental unit has been completed up to date. Likewise, computer programs describing transient rather than equilibrium behaviour are still being refined. Nevertheless, it is already clear that the DCE has particularly favourable characteristics in this respect (Fig. 7). A step input of fuel, in response to a sudden load demand, will result in the first instance in rapid acceleration of the low inertia parts of the system, i.e. the engine and compressor (Figs. 1 and 2). The resultant rapid attainment of high engine power and boost levels favourably reacts on the overall system response compared with a conventional system, in which engine and output-shaft speed are in a fixed ratio, with consequent less rapid pickup of engine power (essentially by turbocharger acceleration only) and distinct danger of overfuelling and heavy smoke emission. The experimental response curves in Fig. 7 clearly illustrate the rapid attainment of high engine speed, boost and hence power levels, followed by more gradual acceleration of the output shaft. The case illustrated corresponds to a vehicle of approximately 20 ton weight being accelerated from 30 mile/h to 40 mile/h, the vehicle having a potential maximum speed of 60 mile/h.

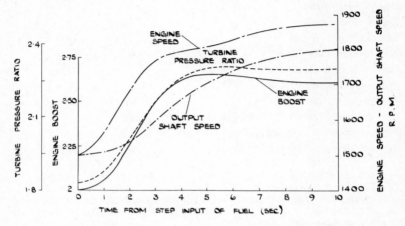

Fig. 7   Transient response of D.C.E. to step input of fuel (52 mm^3/stroke to 105 mm^3/stroke)

Thus the differential connection, coupled with inherently generous trapped-air/fuel ratios under all operating conditions, give the unit a distinct advantage over all alternative transport prime movers.

5   Optimisation of compression ratio and maximum cylinder pressure

The compound engine, as opposed to the turbocharged engine, is particularly flexible in the range of effective compression ratios and maximum cylinder pressures that can be adopted. Thus, if low compression ratios appear attractive from the standpoint of emissions, they can be tolerated more readily than in the turbocharged engine, since starting difficulties are greatly eased by the combination of mechanically driven compressor and variable turbine nozzles, which allows high boost pressures to be attained even during starting. Likewise, the loss of engine efficiency usually associated with low compression ratios and maximum pressures can be offset by the gain in the turbine power contribution due to higher engine exhaust and hence turbine-inlet temperatures.

Figs. 8a-f show the results of extensive computations, all applicable to the high output condition N_e = 2500 rev/min, r_c = 2·75 (see Fig. 5) at an output shaft speed of 2000 rev/min, when both engine volumetric compression ratio and maximum cylinder pressure are systematically varied. A fixed level of engine power is implied by the DCE mode of operation.

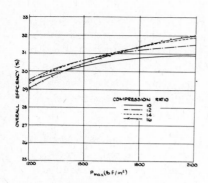

Fig. 8a Overall efficiency as function of P_{max}

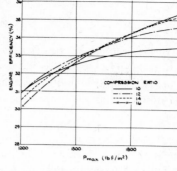

Fig. 8b Engine efficiency as function of P_{max}

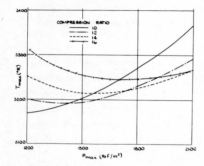

Fig. 8c Maximum cycle temperature

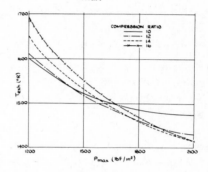

Fig. 8d Exhaust temperature

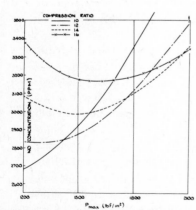

Fig. 8e NO concentration at T_{max}

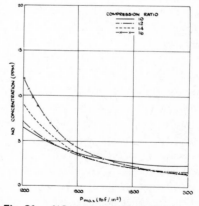

Fig. 8f NO concentration at T_{exh}

Figs. 8a and b show very similar trends for both overall and engine efficiency, the former reflecting the latter in somewhat attenuated form.

Thus the lowest compression ratio (r_{eff} = 10 : 1), except for the lowest maximum cylinder pressure p_{max} = 1200 lbf/in^2, gives very significantly lower efficiencies,

65

whereas the highest compression ratio, starting with an initial disadvantage at p_{max} = 1200 lbf/in^2, leads to substantial gains in efficiency at higher values of p_{max}, the gain in engine efficiency being 2 percentage points at p_{max} = 2100 lbf/in^2. The overall range of engine efficiencies is from 30% (r_{eff} = 16, p_{max} = 1200 lbf/in^2) to 35% (r_{eff} = 16, p_{max} = 2100 lbf/in^2), the corresponding band of overall efficiencies being 29% to 32%. The diminished range of the latter is due to the compensating effect of higher exhaust temperatures at low values of p_{max} (Fig. 8d).

Figs. 8c and d show maximum cylinder temperature T_{max} and exhaust temperature T_{exh}, plotted on the same basis. In the case of the lowest volumetric compression ratio r_{eff} = 10, T_{max} rises sharply by 250°R over the range of p_{max} from 1200 to 2100 lbf/in^2; the opposite trend is observed, though the fall is relatively slight, for the highest compression ratio r_{eff} = 16.

In the case of the exhaust temperature T_{exh}, there is a pronounced decrease with increase in maximum cycle pressure, the rate of decrease being most pronounced for the highest compression ratio r_{eff} = 16.

For both T_{max} and T_{exh}, maximum values at p_{max} = 1200 lbf/in^2 are associated with the highest compression ratio, whereas, at p_{max} = 2100 lbf/in^2, the situation is reversed. This leads to the important conclusion, when taken with the corresponding trends for overall and engine efficiency (Figs. 8a and b) that, where operation at low p_{max} is specifically desired, a low compression ratio should be adopted at the same time, but, if in the interests of best efficiency, a high value of p_{max} is tolerated, a high value of volumetric compression ratio should also be adopted.

The curves for NO concentration at the maximum cycle temperature T_{max} and at the exhaust temperature T_{exh} (Figs. 8e and f, respectively) are almost mirror images of the trends for T_{max} and T_{exh} (Figs. 8c and d). As already stated, they are based on simple equilibrium calculations for 11 species, and are therefore subject to the inevitable limitations of such treatments. In particular, the calculated concentrations at T_{max}, reading 3986 ppm (parts in 10^6) at p_{max} = 2100 lbf/in^2 and r_{eff} = 10, are likely to be considerably pessimistic, since equilibrium can never be reached during the combustion process, although, against this trend, reference must be made to the further limitations of a single-zone combustion treatment. Inevitably, there will be local hot zones where concentrations will be very much higher. However, of low p_{max} = 1200 lbf/in^2, and low r_{eff} = 10 : 1, should be conducive to the lowest possible NO concentrations (2675 ppm, calculated). The calculated equilibrium concentrations at T_{exh}, Fig. 8f, are very low indeed, and do not reflect the well known phenomenon of frozen equilibrium. However, it would seem that, although calculated values in the range 1 − 12 ppm have no absolute significance, the frozen-equilibrium situation normally associated with the spark-ignition engine would not hold fully in the case of the DCE because of the very low values of mixed-exhaust temperature (Table 2) and the relatively long residence times in the exhaust manifold. It is hoped at a later stage to measure NO concentrations in the exhaust manifold, but all the indications are that, with its generous air/fuel ratios and low mixed-exhaust temperatures, the DCE is in a very favourable position. Similar remarks apply also to carbon monoxide and smoke; even at the highest rating at which the unit has been operated experimentally, namely:

Engine speed N_e = 2400 rev/min

Boost-pressure ratio r_c = 2·75

Engine bhp = 235

Engine bmep = 219 lbf/in^2

there is virtually no exhaust smoke.

Summarising, there are clear indications that a combination of low maximum cylinder pressure and low volumetric-compression ratio, which can be more readily accommodated in the DCE than in the turbocharged diesel engine, can very materially improve emission levels, particularly with respect to NO. The beneficial effects of reduced maximum cylinder pressure on combustion noise are well known. Conversely, the efficiency penalty involved in the adoption of low p_{max} and r_{eff} is considerably instigated by the compensating effect of higher exhaust temperature, and hence higher turbine power feedback.

6 Comparisons with other transport prime movers

An attempt to compare the DCE objectively with other existing and potential transport prime movers was made in Reference 5, from which Table 4 is reproduced. Clearly, the most serious contender in the field at the present moment is the high-output turbocharged engine. The remaining units listed in Table 4, namely the vehicle gas turbine (regenerative), and the 2-stage Wankel engine (Reference 7), are still not sufficiently developed to be considered as serious competitors. The points ratings (5 to 1 in descending order of quality) have been fully justified in Reference 5.

Table 4

Prime-mover type	DCE	Turbocharged engine	Gas Turbine	2-stage wankel engine	Stirling engine
Reliability	4	5	3	2	3
Fuel economy	4	5	3	4	3
High unit output					
(i) specific weight	4	3	5	5	2
(ii) bulk	3	3	3	5	2
Torque characteristics	5	3	3	2	3
(i) torque backup	5	3	3	2	3
(ii) braking torque	5	3	4	2	2
(iii) transient response	5	3	2	4	3
Pollution level					
(i) noise	2	3	3	4	5
(ii) emissions	3	2	4	2	5
Costs					
(i) capital (a complexity)	4	5	3	3	2
(ii) maintenance	4	5	3	2	3

The major advantage of the DCE relative to the high-output turbocharged engine lies in the greatly superior torque characteristics (Figs. 4 and 6), where not only inherent torque backup, but also transient response and braking characteristics (by reversed turbine nozzles), are markedly better suited to the traction application. The possibility of stepless transmission, or, at the most, the use of a 2 forward and reverse ratio gearbox, makes the unit particularly attractive for a wide range of transport applications, and justifies the top rating of 5. In other respects, slight penalties have to be paid. With regard to fuel economy, improved compressor design will lead to certain further gain, but, in considering the high-output turbocharged engine, it must be remembered that the adoption of sophisticated semiautomatic or automatic transmission systems will inevitably reduce overall efficiencies very substantially. This applies particularly to multiratio hydrokinetic or split-power hydrostatic transmissions.

With regard to pollution levels, the more flexible operation of the DCE with regard to volumetric compression ratio and maximum cylinder pressure and the inherently generous air/fuel ratios, justify the superior emission rating in Table 4 (the Stirling engine having the best rating), but noise, although readily controllable in the engine itself with the adoption of low maximum cylinder pressures, will be somewhat above the level of the turbocharged engine owing to the high inherent noise level of the Lysholm compressor. Again, the Stirling engine has the best rating, but it must be remembered that this is still far from fully developed, and many of its other features are less attractive.

7 Conclusions

The DCE has many features that make it particularly suitable as a high-output vehicular prime mover. The experimental unit has achieved performance figures broadly in line with theoretical predictions, the major discrepancies being due to excessive epicyclic gearbox losses.

It is considered to have a number of very significant operational advantages over its obvious competitor, the high-output turbocharged diesel engine.

8 Acknowledgements

The authors are indebted to Perkins Engines Ltd. for support of this project, and to the technician staff of the School of Engineering for the successful carrying out of an extensive experimental programme.

9 References

1	WALLACE, F.J.	'Operating characteristics of compound engine schemes for traction purposes based on opposed piston two stroke engines with differential gearing', Proc. IMechE, **178**, (2), 1963
2	WALLACE, F.J.	'The differential compound engine'. SAE, Detroit — 670110, January 1967.
3	WALLACE, F.J., FEW, P.C., and CAVE, P.R.	'The differential compound engine — interim test results and assessment of future development', Proc.IMechE, VHO symposium, Nottingham, Paper 6.
4	WALLACE, F.J., FEW, P.C., and CAVE, P.R.	'The differential compound engine — further development'. SAE Paper 710085, Detroit, January 1971.

5   WALLACE, F.J.   'The differential compound engine' (accepted by IMechE).

6   FELLER, F.   'The two-stage rotary engine — a new concept in diesel power'. Proc. IMechE, 1970-71, **185**, 13/71

7   NEELEN, G.T.M., ORTEGREN, L.G.H. KULLMANN, P., and ZACHARIAS, F.   'Stirling engines in traction applications'. CIMAC 1971, Paper A26.

6 The rotary combustion engine and some of its characteristics

R.F. Ansdale, M.S.A.E., C.Eng., M.I.Mech.E.
Consultant

It is pertinent to take a closer look at the automotive scene and seek an understanding as to why it should be necessary to produce automobile engines for a performance range of 15 or 20 to 400 bhp, or even higher, to transport two to six persons at a time.

Positive-displacement internal-combustion engines have been developed over the years to provide a useful power output over a wide performance range by varying the bmep, the crankshaft speed and/or both within the limits imposed by the respective design. Characteristically, car engines run mostly under part-load and low-bmep, conditions at greatly varying speeds. Volumes could be written about the progress since, say, the first Benz car engine of 1886, which developed 2/3 hp at 250 to 300 rev/min, but was later proved capable of 0·88 hp at a formidable 400 rev/min (see 'The annals of Mercedes-Benz motor-vehicles and engines'), to the 1500 c^3 (90 in^3) BRM, which finally scaled the 400 bhp level at a handsome five-figure rev/min.

Excluding special and racing-car engines, the reliable production 100 bhp unit proved rather elusive for a long time, and maximum engine speeds of 3000 to 3600 rev/min were not at all uncommon in the 1930s, when rebores after 30 000 miles or so were acceptable.

Today, engine speeds are in the up to 6000 rev/min range (12 000 to 14 000 rev/min range for special and racing engines), and motorists expect a life of 100 000 miles. The latter figure is, unfortunately, still not achieved by all motorists or by every type and make of engine.

Driving conditions, driver temperament and other imponderables seem to have determining effects, since mere car size and weight alone fail to account for the differences, or for the need for this exceptionally wide engine-performance range. Perhaps it is safe to assume − rather unscientifically − that the demand for comfort, unobtrusive performance and less vibration, at least up to the legal speed limits, have something to do with it. In addition, automobiles are exported to all corners of the Earth, where they are expected to perform satisfactorily at all altitudes under greatly varying temperature and climatic conditions. It may be recalled tha, when Britain's first motorway, the M1, was opened to the public, many seemingly well maintained cars could not sustain high-speed cruising, and engine speeds would often exceed 5500 rev/min, whereas today a popular overhead-camshaft-engine family car achieves the permissible maximum of a little over 70 mile/h at a comfortable 4000 to 4300 engine rev/min.

The higher up the bhp range we go, the more favourable the figures become, since the greater proportion of engine power output is simply potential power, available for acceleration and for maintaining speeds up gradients, because the specific power requirement, i.e. bhp per ton weight of car, for these purposes does not vary very much. Stylists and others appear to have persuaded manufacturers that nonstreamlined car-body shapes do not entail worthwhile sacrifices.

70

Irrespective of this, it is undoubtedly true that the specific power of a car has determining effects on its performance and on comfort, the advantages increasing relative to the power available. It is interesting to note, and often overlooked, that more powerful cars achieve superior point to point journeys without necessarily using up x times more fuel than a lower-powered vehicle — where x signifies the ratio of power output of the two cars compared. In terms of percentages, the larger engine will run at much lower bmep than smaller engine.

Arguments of this nature indicate that exhaust emissions per vehicle mile, as specified in the American regulations, seem to be an equitable basis for dealing with the emission problem, but are to the detriment of cars with small and medium-size engines.

The very stringent exhaust-emission regulations were triggered off by the peculiarities of geographic and climatic conditions prevailing at Los Angeles in California, which soon found widespread support in the antiautomobile lobby. Car manufacturers had facilitated these moves by apparent oversight and/or complacency in not recognising their rightful obligation in this connection. Today we seem to be confronted by a worldwide overreaction to the issues of exhaust-emission control, only partly due to concern for the future, the rest having apparently been recognised in the corridors of power as an opportunity to circumscribe human activity. Indeed, there was a necessary and rude awakening when legal requirements for permissible emission levels and more stringent car safety rules began to be prescribed by legislators.

Confining this paper to power units, it seems pertinent to compare, by way of example, characteristic emission regulations for 1975 and 1976, bearing in mind that HC and CO emissions of 1973 are already more than 80% below the levels of 1964. In addition, it is proposed to show the officially confirmed emission levels of two models of the Japanese Mazda car, which are powered by twin rotor Wankel RC engines.

Emissions, g/mile

	1964	1975	1976	Mazda cars RX3	RX4
Hydrocarbon (HC)	24·0	0·41	0·41	0·21	0·31
Carbon Monoxide (CO)	125·0	3·40	3·40	1·79	2·50
Nitrogen Oxides (NO_x)	6·0	3·00	0·40	0·99	1·46

Precise performance cycles are laid down for these emission tests, and the control devices must have a safe life of 50 000 miles or five years, whichever is the shorter, a bone of contention at present being that, according to the regulations, every car ought to comply with the limits, whereas automakers, quite understandably, suggest testing only one vehicle in every 100, 500 or even 1000 cars rolling off their assembly lines.

However much understanding we may have for the manufacturers' point of view, their request would seem to jeopardise the purpose of the clean-air legislation, besides depriving the motorist of greater assurance that every car he purchases has no excess pollution, but does, in fact, develop approximately the specified power.

Undoubtedly, the scene is set by growing demands for less pollution, matched by the motorist's demand that there should be no sacrifice of performance and reliability — not forgetting that, at long last, people are beginning to ask for how much longer man may continue to use up natural resources at ever increasing rates, that is in general, and not only natural fuel reserves. It is in this sphere that rotary-combustion engines seem capable of making a notable contribution, since they may be 30 − 50% lighter than equal-power reciprocating-piston engines built for the same applications. Moreover, further savings are feasible, as will be elaborated below.

71

The quest for purely rotary prime movers is probably as old as man's dream of emulating the flight of birds. Here's Aeolopile – a turbine concept of the early Christian era, suggests this. Historians delving into the histories of ancient civilisations may conceivably come up with more significant facts, but, for present practical purposes, the history of rotary piston pumps, compressors and/or power units begins with Ramelli (1588), Thomas Newcombe, and James Watt (1736-1819), who, with his companions, sought rotary engine configurations when the principles of the beam engine met with scepticism from their contemporaries. Nor has the reciprocating piston-engine principle for steam and internal-combustion engines been completely accepted, as searches through technical literature and Patent Office files reveal. The actual 4-stroke cycle was suggested by a French civil engineer, Alphonse Beau de Rochas, in 1862, while engineers were concentrating on the Lenoir cycle, which lacked a compression phase and was therefore doomed to yield very low thermal efficiencies.

Dr. N.A. Otto, a German engineer, invented his 4-stroke engine in 1876. At that time, there were already so many rotary engine configurations under consideration or development that Prof. F. Reuleaux attempted to sort out the chaos. This confusion has arisen because it is possible to think of countless different basic configurations, most of which could be executed in several different ways. The creators of these rotary piston machines appeared only too ready to switch from configuration to configuration instead of putting sound engineering into their more promising designs.

Charles Parsons is also among the notable engineers who produced a successful rotary steam engine in 1882 before being absorbed in turbine work, but perhaps the most successful early rotary-combustion engine was designed by Seguin in 1907 as a radial aircraft engine, which gained fame as the Gnome le Rhone aeroengine during the First World War.

Nor was inventive ingenuity stifled by the phenomenal success of the reciprocating-piston engine achieved since the First World War. This success seems to be based on better materials, rapidly advancing production techniques and better appreciation of thermodynamics.

The first notable challenge to reciprocating-piston engines came with the introduction of jet and turbojet engines, followed in 1957-58 by the now famous Wankel RC engine, the first modern positive-displacement rotary-combustion engine capable of outperforming the conventional piston engine, demanding fewer raw materials and less labour to manufacture. Most significantly, its NO_x emissions amount to barely 50% of those of an equal-output, equal-compression-ratio reciprocating-piston engine. Unfortunately, its base emissions of HC and CO are somewhat higher than for an equivalent reciprocating-piston engine.

Let it be said right at the beginning that, contrary to popular belief, the surface/volume ratio, the importance of which is greatly overrated, does not have an overall determining effect.

So far, emission data available was obtained from engines relying on carburettors; very different results may be anticipated when fuel injection, i.e. the right kind of fuel-injection equipment, is used.

The emission phenomena of the Wankel RC engine need explanation. Published data suggest that combustion in a Wankel RC engine may be relatively slow; however, it is certain that exhaust temperatures are sufficiently high to sustain combustion within a suitable chamber if adequate oxygen is present and/or injected. It is also a peculiarity of this configuration that flame propagation is relatively slow even in a moving gas, hence there is quite a wedge of unburned hydrocarbons on the trailing side of every chamber. When, therefore, the adjacent apex seal begins to uncover the exhaust port, hot gases will issue at a fair rate, causing sufficiently low pressure to draw in unburned hydrocarbon from ahead of the seal.

However large the problem may loom to those unaccustomed to dealing with Wankel RC engines, there is no doubt that the emission paradox of this engine is easier to solve, and it readily yields to the same techniques as reciprocating piston engines. Furthermore, as the NSU/Wankel RC engine runs on regular grade petrol, it avoids any lead-emission problems.

Second generation of rotary-combustion engines

Dr. Felix Wankel himself recognised the countless alternative rotary-engine configurations that could be devised, even without taking into account the so-called intersecting-axis engines, which are difficult to draw and analyse because the essential variable volumes are formed by one or other major component performing complex motions in three planes.

Whichever way one looks at the status quo, it is difficult to believe that no other type of rotary-combustion engine can be devised that will be capable of challenging the reciprocating-piston engine as well as the Wankel concept. Indeed, serious work is in progress in Germany on at least two different concepts. One is Prof. Huf's, which is being sponsored by an aircraft company, and the other appears to be a 'cat-and-mouse' design — one of very many — on which considerable sums of money have been spent, without much chance of success. Two cat-and-mouse designs are under development in the USA, and another is doing the rounds in the UK. Cat-and-mouse designs are so called because they usually contain two rotors which move at variable angular velocity to form variable volume chambers between them, and which are capable of accommodating a sensible thermodynamic cycle. Most ingenious devices from oval and square gears to bell cranks and connecting rods, as well as Hooks joints, have been suggested for ensuring the correct angular velocities of the rotors. Designs of cat-and-mouse engines present considerable inertia problems, some imposing additional gas loads with predictable results. Inventors do not seem to appreciate that dynamic sealing grids, as needed for most rotary-combustion engines, work satisfactorily only between two moving parts or between one moving part — the rotor — and a stationary part — the casing. When there are two or more moving parts, sealing contact has to jump from component to component, usually leaving a leakage path. Some rotary-combustion engines examined incorporate the worst of both worlds; for example, the Huf engine in Germany incorporates not only a rotary-combustion engine sealing grid but also poppet valves, which are known to impose limitations on reciprocating-piston engines.

Clarke, Walker and Hamilton from the NGTE demonstrated the feasibility of an intersecting axis nutating piston engine design; they presented their findings in a paper to the Institution of Mechanical Engineers. They worked thoroughly through the mathematics of their complex design, and some sealing and rotor cooling matters seem to have been left for attention in the future.

Although this engine has not been designed or developed into a viable commercial product, it does make a notable contribution to rotary-combustion engine knowledge.

The writer was privileged to examine another intersecting axis nutating piston engine configuration very similar to the above some years ago. Indeed, it appeared superior in some respects, but it was not proceeded with when it was realised that estimated development costs were decidedly discouraging. This design too was the work of an Englishman resident in Australia at the time.

The writer has also been privileged to be closely associated with the design and development of the ANIDYNE engine, which takes advantage of both reciprocating-piston and rotary-combustion engine know-how. Fundamentally this design aims at producing an inherently low-pollution rotary-combustion engine, and at least theoretical considerations suggest the feasibility of its achievement.

As the illustration shows, the Anidyne engine must be clearly defined as a planetary-rotation device with intermeshing engagement. Moreover, it is a completely balanced unit in which two double-ended pistons rotate about their own respective centre of gravity, which in turn orbits in a perfect circle round the output-shaft centre. As the shaft is offset from the rotor centre exactly by the eccentricity of its eccentric portions, which control piston movement, the total stroke amounts to four times the eccentricity. Being completely balanced, the engine runs practically vibration-free. According to the illustration, two double-ended pistons move within the same plane in their respective bores in a semispherical rotor. One of the pistons induces air before partially compressing it and transferring it to the power cylinder, where final compression takes place. Fuel is injected and burnt. Expansion follows until the exhaust port opens, and the sequence of operations is repeated. This sequence, as described, necessitates the shaft turning at twice rotor speed; both move at constant angular velocity, and shaft and rotor may be geared together for certain applications, though this is thought to be superfluous for small and medium-size engines and compressors now under development.

Gas-flow conditions are perhaps more readily appreciated if the rotor is divided into three zones; the centre-portion width is determined by the diameter of the peripheral sealing rings round each end of the power-cylinder bore. The outlet of the transfer port, fuel injection, sparking plug and exhaust port are arranged round the housing within this cone. To one side of this central zone is the inlet zone, and, on the other, the transfer zone. The sealing grid separates the zones from each other, and isolates the inside of the engine from the gases.

All peripheral sealing elements rub against the semispherical surface of the casing bore, thus minimising differential thermal expansion and other problems.

For reasons that have become less convincing, the first prototype engines are running with rectangular air-pumping pistons, which, in fact, give a reasonable account of themselves, and which permitted the use of minimum rotor size.

The semispherical rotor and casing configuration was chosen because it was possible to arrange that all peripheral sealing elements are either complete sealing rings or circular-arc sealing strips. Moreover, spherical surfaces present no particular manufacturing problems, and chatter marks, such as plagued the Wankel RC engine early in its life, cannot form. So far, no reasons have been found why the spherical rotor should be abandoned in favour of other shapes.

As indicated earlier, the Anidyne engine was conceived as an inherently low pollution engine. To date it cannot be said that this aim has been achieved, because development work in progress is concentrating on various mechanical features, and on overall performance. After the desired performance and reliability have been achieved, the issue of exhaust emission will be tackled.

It is thus emphasised that this part of the paper is so far unsupported by any test data, but, to our engineering team, it seems more important to endeavour to develop an advanced concept than to create merely another rotary-combustion engine. The men and the means have been made available to bring this research and development work to a successful conclusion.

Fundamentally, the design simply takes advantage of the separate air pump, which can be suitably proportioned to take into account spill losses while the opening periods of the transfer and exhaust ports overlap. Some of these spill losses may be deliberately bled off for pollution control. First, air can be blown into the exhaust port for afterburning purposes without having provided a separate air pump. Of greater significance is the facility of air or mixture injection directly into the power cylinder at a suitable moment during the expansion phase, decidedly before the exhaust port opens, the purpose being to initiate secondary combustion. It is expected that completing the combustion process as described will not cause temperatures so high that additional NO_x is developed.

It has not been possible to make a comprehensive weight analysis of the Anidyne engine, and compare it with that of a conventional engine, but, if engine bulk is indicative, a very favourable weight should be achieved that is not far short of the weight of the equivalent output Wankel RC engine. In addition, it has already been confirmed that impressively low man hours are required for the manufacture of the Anidyne engine. For instance, the single-rotor prototype engine is assembled in no more than 15 min.

This paper convers a wide field, because it was thought necessary to put the record straight, and show that rotary-combustion engines are not a momentary fad. There is a decided need for them, since new and expected regulations concerning exhaust emissions and safety requirements can only be satisfied with conventional engines at considerable sacrifice. As shown above, rotary-combustion engines can comply with these regulations, besides promising notable advantages in other directions.

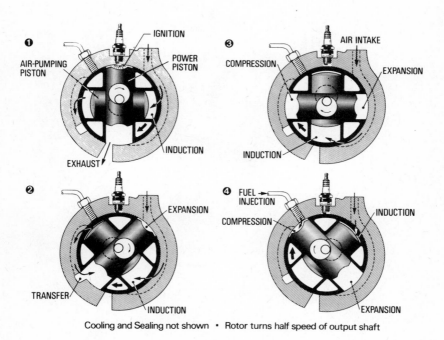

Cooling and Sealing not shown • Rotor turns half speed of output shaft

Fig. 1   Operation of Anidyne engine

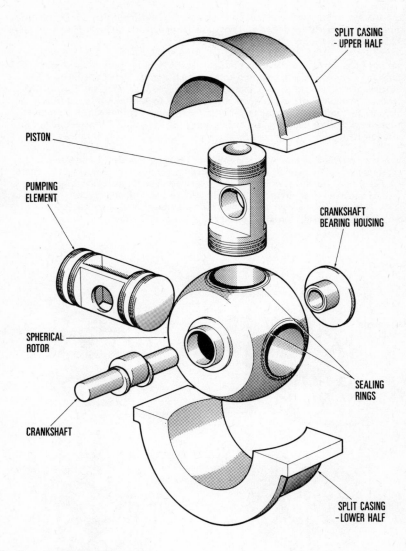

SPLIT CASING
- UPPER HALF

PISTON

PUMPING
ELEMENT

CRANKSHAFT
BEARING HOUSING

SPHERICAL
ROTOR

SEALING
RINGS

CRANKSHAFT

SPLIT CASING
- LOWER HALF

Fig. 2   Anidyne compressor

Part 3

Continuous combustion engines

7 The automotive gas turbine

Prof. R.S. Fletcher, B.Sc.Tech., D.I.C., Ph.D.
Cranfield Institute of Technology, Cranfield, England

1 Introduction

The gas turbine first found application in the automobile in 1949, when the Rover Company installed a 100 hp engine in a mobile test frame. Not many years later, in 1953, Chrysler Corporation of the USA produced its first gas-turbine-powered automobile and demonstrated its capabilities on the streets of Detroit. Both companies continued to explore the potential of the engine, but neither developed a production engine. The Rover Company, as Rover Gas Turbines, went on to produce a range of engines from 60 hp to 140 hp, which found application as auxiliary power units in aircraft systems, and perhaps its finest achievement occurred in 1965, when one of its engines propelled the first British car over the line in the 24 h race at Le Mans. The car was placed tenth overall, but did perform with a better fuel consumption than any other in the race. Chrysler produced 50 experimental cars in 1963, which suffered from a lag in acceleration and poor low-speed fuel-consumption characteristics relative to the spark-ignition engines. These cars were loaned to many drivers over a period of years, however, and the reactions found to be favourable. The Rover Gas Turbine expertise is now focused on turbine engines of greater than 350 hp, but Chrysler continues to explore systems in the lower hp range. Ford Motor and General Motor companies of the USA currently sell production gas-turbine engines of approximately 350 hp for application in trucks, but attention will be focused in this paper on smaller engine systems.

Interest in the gas-turbine engine for automotive application in the 100-200 hp output range has grown rapidly in recent years, and most of the larger motor companies throughout the world are aggressively developing such engines. Its potential as a lightweight, reliable, long-lived power source, coupled with the aesthetic and practical appeal of using nonreciprocating machinery, has long been recognised, as it was these features that attracted the interest shown in the early years. The growth in interest over recent years, however, has arisen out of the concern for the pollutant levels developed by piston-engined automobiles as has been reflected in the pollution-control legislation currently in force in the USA. Gas turbines have the potential of producing significantly lower emissions of pollutants, as the combustion process is both continuous and occurs at lower levels of temperature and pressure than is the case for the piston engine.

Further development work is required, however, to realise the full potential of the gas turbine in the power range of interest. Current gas-turbine engines exhibit what is considered to be unacceptably high fuel-consumption characteristics at low-power-level operating conditions, the levels of oxides of nitrogen in the engine exhaust exceed the stated US control standards for 1976, and there is still no clear picture as to the relative economics in operation of the gas-turbine and piston engines. The object of this paper is to consider these factors and others that limit acceptance of the gas turbine, to relate them to the current state of the art in gas-turbine design practice, and to isolate those development activities that may best serve to make the gas-turbine engine an even more competitive and pollution-free power system.

2. Performance characteristics

An attempt will be made to relate the fuel consumption and power output characteristics of gas turbine engines to their inherent thermodynamic and the present-day mechanical limitations. A full rigorous treatment will not be attempted, as such information is readily available in standard texts (Reference 1), but attention will be focused on those specific limitations that affect the small, automobile-size, gas turbine. The limitations and performance of the combustion system will be considered separately in the Section 3 and given special attention as it controls the all-important pollution characteristics of the engine. The thermodynamic and mechanical limitations will be considered separately.

2.1 Gas turbine cycles

The gas turbine in its most simple form comprises a compressor, a combustor and a turbine linked to the compressor by means of a shaft (Fig. 1). In operation, the shaft rotates, the compressor increases the kinetic energy of the air, which diffuses to the top

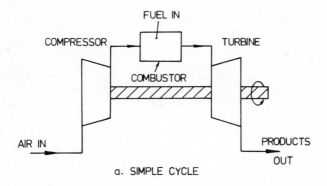

a. SIMPLE CYCLE

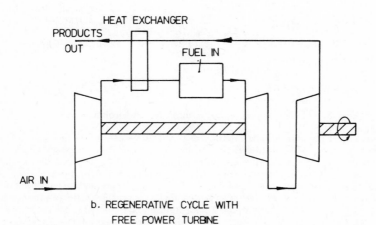

b. REGENERATIVE CYCLE WITH
FREE POWER TURBINE

Fig. 1   Gas-turbine cycles

operating pressure at which fuel is burned at constant pressure conditions to increase further the kinetic energy of the air. The high-pressure, high-velocity combustion products then drive the turbine and the surplus energy delivered to the shaft, over that required by the compressor, is available to do work.

The simple cycle has the obvious appeal of having very few components, but it has limitations in automotive-type applications, where shaft power is required over a wide range of power and speed levels. Compressor performance characteristics are very sensitive to both changes, and its adiabatic efficiency decreases rapidly at off-design conditions to a point at which the compressor fails to function at all. These limitations may be overcome by operating with two separate turbines, with the first driving the compressor and the second developing the required shaft power. Mechanically this is easy to achieve, and it allows the gas generator (as the components without the power turbine are called) to operate at a more constant speed condition closer to the full-power condition. Further modifications may be made to this cycle to improve thermodynamic efficiency. As the exhaust temperature normally exceeds the combustor-inlet temperature, energy can be recovered by heat exchange between these gas streams. Intercoolers may also be employed between stages in the compression process, and additional fuel may be added between the two turbines. All such modifications, however, increase the complexity and costs of the engine system. Detailed calculations of the relative merits of these cycles indicate that the best cycle compromise between complexity and efficiency for the automotive gas turbine is that shown in Fig. 1a, which employs heat recovery and a free power turbine. This cycle is called the regenerative, free power turbine cycle (RFTC), and has been selected by most engine manufacturers for their automobile-development programmes. A typical automotive-engine layout of the RFTC engine is shown schematically in Fig. 2. Debate about the relative merits of the RFTC still persists, but, before this point is considered in more detail, the relative thermodynamic merits of this cycle will be compared with the simple cycle of Fig. 1b.

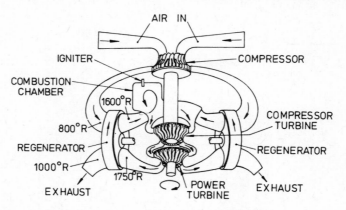

Fig. 2   Schematic of typical automotive gas-turbine engine

Separation of the two turbine functions does not, of course, affect the cycle thermodynamics, and only the degree of heat exchange between the compressed air and expanded combustion products produces any change in characteristics. For the simple cycle, operated at fixed component efficiencies and ambient conditions, the efficiency defined as specific fuel consumption (SFC, lb fuel per hp-h), and the specific power (SP, hp per lb air per s), are characterised by the cycle pressure ratio and the top working temperature, i.e. the turbine entry temperature (TET). For the RFTC cycle, the heat-echanger effectiveness, defined as the percentage of maximum heat transfer possible in terms of the compressor exit and exhaust gas temperatures, also influences the cycle performance. Results of such cycle calculations have been taken from the literature

(Reference 2), in which the following assumptions were made: compressor and turbine polytropic efficiencies of 90%; combustion efficiency of 98%; total pressure losses in the intake, the combustor, the regenerator, and the exhaust ducting equivalent to 7·5% and 17·5% of the cycle-pressure ratio for the simple and regenerative cycles, respectively; and ambient conditions of standard atmospheric pressure and 100°F.

The compressor and turbine efficiencies assumed here are somewhat better than the current state of the art can achieve, but the influence of reduced efficiencies on the calculations will be considered later.

The results shown in Fig. 3 compare, over a wide operating range, the SFC and SP characteristics of the simple cycle, and of the RFTC cycle when it operates with a heat-exchanger effectiveness of 0·9. The range in attainable values of specific fuel consumption is wide, and should be compared with the SFC values of the spark-ignition engine at approximately 0·45, and the diesel engine at approximately 0·40. The following points are noteworthy:

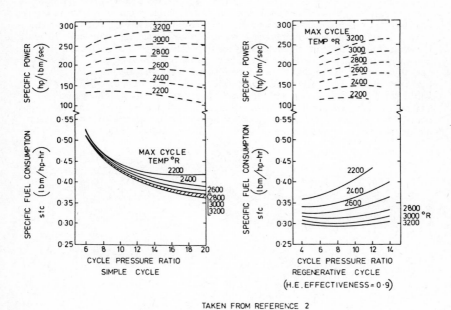

TAKEN FROM REFERENCE 2

Fig. 3   Gas-turbine cycle performance characteristics as function of pressure ratio

(a) An SFC of 0·35 is only attainable from a simple cycle if it operates in the pressure ratios well in excess of 20:1 and TET values greater than 3200° R.

(b) Regenerative cycles with a heat-exchanger effectiveness of 0·90 will operate at an SFC of 0·35, or lower, if the pressure ratio is between 3:1 and 9:1 and if the TET value exceeds 2400° R.

(c) The specific power output of the regenerative cycle is approximately 10% lower than that of the simple cycle.

In summary, therefore, the regenerative cycle from a thermodynamic point of view is clearly the superior cycle as it offers a fuel-consumption characteristic at the design point that is appreciably better than that for the simple-cycle gas turbine and for conventional reciprocating engines.

2.2 Practical limitations

2.2.1 Full power operation

The cycle analyses show that low fuel consumption can be achieved in a regenerative gas turbine if the pressure ratio is between 3:1 and 9:1, and if the turbine entry temperature is equal to 2400° R. Such operating conditions are readily achievable in simple-cycle engines as demonstrated in present-day civilian aircraft systems which operate to ratios of 25:1 and with TET values up to 3000° R. The one significant difference between the aircraft engine and the regenerative engine is, of course, the inlet temperature to the combustor (CIT); owing to the exhaust-heat recovery in the latter case, its CIT value is increased over that of the simple cycle for a set-pressure-ratio engine. It is this increase in temperature that improves the specific fuel consumption, and, as first shown in Reference 2, it is the value of the com bustor-inlet temperature that controls the SFC characteristics for the regenerative cycle. This can be demonstrated by replotting the data of Fig. 3 with a change in abscissa to combustor-inlet temperature. The result of this change, given in Fig. 4, shows that an SFC of 0·35 corresponds with a CIT value of approximately 1600° R, and an SFC of 0·30 with a value of 1950° R. The state of the art in aircraft-engine technology calls for CIT values of approximately 1500° R; so it can be seen that, to realise the full potential of the regenerative engine, it is necessary to operate the combustor at significantly higher values of inlet temperatures than is present in aircraft engines.

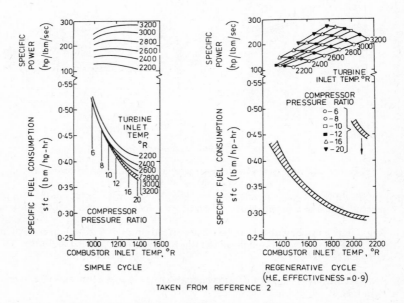

Fig. 4   Gas-turbine cycle performance characteristics as function of combustor inlet temperature

82

The air that enters a gas-turbine combustor both feeds the main combustion zone and serves to cool the combustor liner. As the inlet temperature increases, its cooling capability decreases, hence liner-wall temperatures also increase, unless more cooling air is added (Reference 3). Current operational technology is limited by combustor-material durability problems to CIT values of approximately 1700° R, and, although this is sufficient to obtain an acceptable SFC at design point, Fig. 4 shows that a 10% improvement can be obtained for a further 300° R increase in CIT. As is also shown in Fig. 4, turbine entry temperature does not limit the SFC, but it does influence greatly the specific power, and therefore the engine weight and size. The current operating limit of approximately 3000° R in TET is more than sufficient for the regenerative engine, but it does require at present the use of expensive materials and manufacturing techniques. Further improvements in technology are also necessary at the hot end of the engine, therefore, if the full potential in engine size is to be attained.

2.2.2 Part-power operation

The discussion so far has been concerned mostly with the performance characteristics at the design, or maximum power, operating point. Automobile engines operate most of their time away from this point; so it is necessary to consider the change in SFC characteristics when the engine operates at part-load conditions. Typical performance characteristics of a conventional gas-turbine engine, and of the piston engines, are shown in Fig. 5. The gas-turbine engine demonstrates the greatest rate of increase in SFC as the power output drops below the maximum, but the relative changes do not become significant until the level reduces below 30% of full power. At 20% full power, the gas-turbine engine has an SFC nearly twice that of the other two engines compared, and, below this, its SFC rises very rapidly. The reasons for the rapid deterioration relate to the change in operating efficiencies of the components as the air mass flow reduces. The effect on turbine operating characteristics is similar to that for compressors, as discussed in Section 2.1, and its effect on the combustor characteristics is considered in Section 3. Both for the turbine and for the compressor, the decrease in efficiency relates to the change in approach velocity of the air. The ideal engine would be designed with a variable working annulus area so that, say, 10% power could be obtained with the engine operating at its design point in terms of the thermodynamic properties and characteristic velocities, but at 10% of the maximum mass flow rate. Such a concept is pursued and variable area nozzles are introduced upstream of the turbine and compressor (Reference 4), but clearly there is a limit to this approach, as it introduces complexity both in manufacture and control.

An alternative method of improving part-load SFC characteristics is to employ a differential gear system (Reference 5) that permits the compressor speed to remain more nearly constant even when the power-turbine speed varies from zero to the maximum operating speed. Effectively, this approach reduces the rate of decline in compressor and turbine efficiencies as the power output decreases. General Motors has used a similar power-transfer system in their GT309 gas turbine (Reference 6), and it is interesting to note the change in combustor-inlet temperature that occurs as the engine operates over its full range. Data of this characteristic, shown in Fig. 6 and taken from Reference 7, indicates that the value of CIT first increases from approximately 1600° R to 1750° R with decreasing power and that it never drops below 1450° R even at idle. The results of Fig. 4 imply that this engine must have very good off-design SFC characteristics. It is also noteworthy that the compressor turbine never drops below 55% of the maximum power output level — a factor that ensures that the lag in acceleration response time is considerably improved on that exhibited by the early Chrysler engines.

83

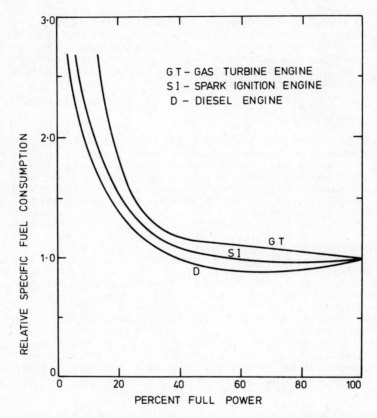

Fig. 5 Typical part-load operating characteristic of gas-turbine, diesel and spark-ignition engines

84

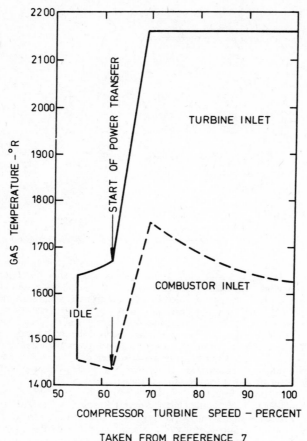

Fig. 6   Operating conditions of General Motors GT-309 combustor

2.2.3   Component efficiencies

The assumptions made concerning component efficiencies in calculating the results given in Fig. 3 and 4 are believed to reflect the current state of the art for all components except the compressor. The assumption of 90% polytropic efficiency for this component contradicts the current practice of achieving approximately 85% for 4:1 pressure-ratio systems. The computations have been repeated therefore at this condition, and the results are compared with the previous ones in Table 1.

The effect of this change is shown to degrade both fuel consumption and specific power performance by approximately 10%, but to maintain these characteristics at acceptable levels. A significant recovery in performance can be obtained with higher values of regenerator effectiveness, but this can only be achieved at present at the expense of increasing the size and weight of the regenerator to intolerable levels.

Table 1

Compressor efficiency versus cycle performance

CIT	SFC(A)	SFC(B)	SP(A)	SP(B)
°R	lb/hp-h		hp per lb per s	
1600	0·34	0·37	170	155
1750	0·32	0·34	155	140
1900	0·30	0·32	120	110

A condition: Compressor polytropic efficiency = 90%
B condition: Compressor polytropic efficiency = 85%
Pressure ratio in range 3:1 to 9:1
TET = 2600° R

2.3 Current engines and future developments to improve specific fuel consumption

It is instructive to compare some of the gas-turbine engines that have so far been developed, or considered, and which may find application as automotive engines, both with each other and with the data presented above. Such engine systems are given in Table 2. All four engines concepts pursued by the automotive-engine manufacturers, Chrysler, General Motors, Rover and Volvo, are shown to be regenerative with a free power turbine, and the similarity in the engines operating characteristics is striking. All operate at a pressure ratio close to 4:1 and with a turbine entry temperature near to 2100° R. The fuel-consumption characteristics do not reach the value of 0·35 lb/hph, which was the reference value considered above owing to the relative inefficiencies of the compressor and turbine systems. The Volvo engine SFC is quoted to be 0·4, and is significantly better than that for the other three engines.

The fifth system given in Table 1, the United Aircraft Research Laboratories SSS-12 engine, has characteristics that are in direct contrast to that of the other four. It is nominally a 12:1 pressure ratio, simple-cycle concept, as shown by Fig. 1a, which is at present only at the conceptual phase, and it reflects the current state of the art in aerospace technology. It is claimed (Reference 9) that such an engine would be competitive in terms of overall automobile operating economics both with regenerative and with free-turbine engines. The improved fuel consumption that accompanies regeneration is negated, it is calculated, by the costs of the regenerator over a 4-year, 50 000-mile engine life, and that the free turbine can be replaced with alternative transmission systems that might incorporate 8-speed gear systems. These results are the subject of considerable debate. It appears unlikely, however, that future engines will be developed without regenerators, as the UARL study itself shows the improvement in fuel economy that can be achieved with them is considerable. The results (Fig. 7) show that a simple-cycle gas-turbine engine can perform at 14 mile/gal,*whereas a 7:1, regenerative cycle can operate at 21 mile/gal over a (UARL) typical operating cycle which compares very favourably with the 15 mile/gal quoted for a typical US spark-ignition engine. It is noteworthy also that regenerator effectiveness was assumed to be less than 50% for the regenerated-cycle calculations. Clearly increased effectiveness, repeat calculations for longer engine life, and the concern for fuel conservation, will together dictate the need for the presence of a regenerator in gas-turbine automobile engines.

*US gal

Table 2

Operating characteristics of some automobile gas turbines

Characteristic	Chrysler (A-831)	GM (GT-305)	Rover (2S/140)	Volvo	UACL SSS-12
Rated output, bhp	130	225	150	250	150
Compressor ratio	4:1	3·5:1	3·9:1	4·25:1	11·1:1
Compressor efficiency at full load, %	80	78	79	82	78
Compressor-turbine efficiency, %	87	84	86	86	88
2nd-stage turbine efficiency, %	84	81	86	86	None
Regenerator or heat exchanger effectiveness, %	90	86	78	85	None
Compressor-turbine speed, maximum rev/min	44,600	33,000	65,000	43,000	–
2nd-stage turbine speed, rev/min	45,700	27,000	36,000	43,000	None
Inlet temperature, deg R	2,167	2,057	1,998	2,022	2,410
Airflow, lb/s	2·2	3·5	2·15	3·01	1·06
Specified fuel consumption, lb/hph	0·51	0·535	0·55	0·401	0·51
		REGENERATIVE			NON-REG.

Notes:

(a)   Regenerative engine data from Reference 8

(b)   UACL engine data from Reference 9

(c)   Add 3% to quoted compressor efficiency to obtain approximate polytropic values, and subtract 1% for turbines

In summary, therefore, it has been shown that the two areas that most need to be developed to reduce the fuel-consumption characteristics of potential automotive gas turbines are:

(a)   methods of increasing the combustor inlet temperature

(b)   methods of improving the engine-component efficiencies at part-load conditions

The development of the variable-geometry systems and/or the alternative transmission systems considered above will probably be sufficient to improve part-load characteristics to acceptable levels. The most gain in performance can be obtained, of course, if the maximum-power fuel efficiency can be improved significantly, as this in turn influences the off-design values. Fig. 4 clearly shows that this can only be accomplished with an increase in the combustor-inlet temperature, and, as the present systems operate at the limit of the combustor materials currently available, this will require that new materials are developed. The most interesting materials that are currently under study are the ceramics, and, of these, silicon nitride appears to offer the promise of operation at temperatures as high as 3000°R without any wall cooling (References 10 and 11). It also offers the potential for providing the means of developing such components as variable nozzle guide vanes and turbine blades at costs significantly lower than is the practice today. The importance of this material to these components is not limited to cost, as it will also allow higher turbine-operating temperatures, hence increases in

87

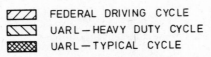

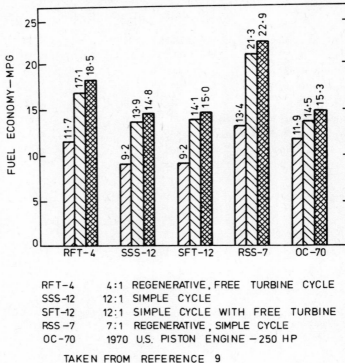

RFT-4	4:1	REGENERATIVE, FREE TURBINE CYCLE
SSS-12	12:1	SIMPLE CYCLE
SFT-12	12:1	SIMPLE CYCLE WITH FREE TURBINE
RSS-7	7:1	REGENERATIVE, SIMPLE CYCLE
OC-70	1970	U.S. PISTON ENGINE - 250 HP

TAKEN FROM REFERENCE 9

Fig. 7   Fuel economy compared with engine-cycle characteristics

specific power and, therefore, much smaller engines for any given power output. An increase to 3000°R, from present-day values of 2100°R at turbine entry, will have the effect of doubling the developed horsepower or halving the engine size (Fig. 4).

The gains to be achieved in terms of SFC, engine size and costs for the small gas turbine are clearly considerable, and the conclusions obtained from the test programmes described in Reference 11 may result in the development of gas turbines of size even smaller than those considered here.

3 Pollutant emission characteristics

The pollutant-emission levels of current gas-turbine combustors are considered and related to their design and operating characteristics. All pollutant species are briefly considered, but particular attention is paid to the oxides of nitrogen, as it will be shown in Section 3.1 that it is this species that will prove to be the most difficult to reduce to the levels required in the current US pollutant standards.

3.1 Pollutant species of concern

There are at least ten products emitted by a gas-turbine combustor that are considered to be undesirable in someway, and hence considered to be pollutants. These products and their undesirable characteristics are given in Table 3.

Table 3

Air pollutants from gas-turbine combustors (Reference 12)

	Pollutant species	Primary effects
1	Carbon monoxide (CO)	Toxic, reduces oxygen capacity of blood
2	Oxides of nitrogen (NO, NO_2)	Toxic, photochemical smog precursor, reduction of visibility
3	Hydrocarbons	Depends on particular composition: can be relatively inert (CH_4), photochemical smog precursors ('reactive hydrocarbons'), toxic (carcinogens)
4	Oxides of sulphur (SO_2, SO_3)	Toxic, aerosol formation
5	Smoke, particulates	Visibility reduction, soiling, plume visibility, possible carriers of toxic materials, nucleation sites, possible weather modification
6	Oxygenated hydrocarbons (aldehydes)	Irritants, odourants, photochemical smog precursors
7	Metals (Mn, V, Na, P, etc.)	Toxic, atmospheric reactions
8	Sulphur component (H_2S, mercaptans)	Toxic, odourants
9	Halogen compounds (HCl, etc.)	Toxic, atmospheric reactions
10	Odourants	Olfactory

The degree of concern that currently exists varies greatly for the pollutants listed. The five pollutants of greatest concern, and for which current legislation exists, are carbon monoxide (CO), the hydrocarbons (HC), the oxides of nitrogen (NO_x), the particulates (which, for gas turbine engines, is mostly smoke) and sulphur dioxide.

The remaining five pollutants will be ignored for the purpose of this paper, but they should not be forgotten, as it is possible that legislation will be brought into force to control some of these pollutants in the not too distant future.

Gas-turbine emission levels of the main five pollutants have been measured from many engine systems over recent years. The results are summarised in Table 4 and compared with typical values from spark-ignition engines and with the US Auto Standard for 1976.

Table 4

Typical engine emission characteristics versus the 1976 US Automobile Standard, g/kg-of-fuel

	CO	HC	NO (as NO_2)	Part*	SO_2
SI uncontrolled (fixed operating cycle)	350	50	25	2	1
GT uncontrolled					
Idle	100	10	2	<1	1
Full-power	1	<1	15	1·5	1
US Auto Standard (approx.)	12	1·5	1·5	–	–

*Particulates for the gas turbine are taken to be carbon only

It should be noted that the present-day gas-turbine engine at full power has CO and HC emissions that are significantly better than the required standards. The nitric-oxide emission level, however, is approximately an order of magnitude higher than the standard called for.

3.2 Design and flow characteristics of a gas-turbine combustor

A satisfactory gas-turbine combustor is one that increases the temperature of an inflowing airstream and at the same time exhibits the following performance requirements;

(i)   high combustion efficiency

(ii)   good combustion stability

(iii)   good temperature-traverse quality at the combustor exit

(iv)   low pressure loss

(v)   ease of ignition

(vi)   low emissions of pollutants

(vii)   durability

(viii) acceptable size

The design problem is one of compromise between these performance criteria in terms of their quantitative values both at the design point and at the off-design points. The present-day conventional gas-turbine combustor has flow characteristics as shown schematically in Fig. 8. It has been evolved over the years with all the above performance criteria in view, with the exception of the requirement for low pollutant emissions. CO and HC have always been considered at the maximum-power operating condition, because their presence is a result of combustion inefficiency, but even these species have been allowed to be present in substantial quantity at the idle operating condition. There are good reasons for this, but before discussing the mechanisms by which these

90

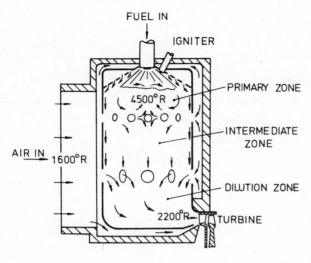

FUEL IN

IGNITER

PRIMARY ZONE

4500°R

INTERMEDIATE ZONE

AIR IN 1600°R

DILUTION ZONE

2200°R TURBINE

Fig. 8   Schematic of typical automotive gas-turbine combustor

pollutants are formed, the flow processes depicted in Fig. 8 will be described in more detail and their characteristics related to the remaining eight performance criteria.

The Figure clearly defines three separate zones – the primary, the intermediate and the dilution – and each has a distinct function to serve. The primary is usually the hottest zone in the combustor, and is the zone where fuel and air are injected at approximately stoichiometric-mixture strength to achieve good stability, ease of ignition and acceptable size. The fuel is usually sprayed from an atomising fuel nozzle, and strategically located jets cause the incoming air to generate the recirculating flow shown in the Figure. It is a region of intense turbulent combustion. The intermediate zone represents a transition between the primary and dilution zones. Mixing occurs in this zone between the heterogeneous products from the primary zone and the entering secondary combustion air, which, in practice, is added sufficiently slowly to permit burnup of any fuel or partially oxidised products that leave the primary zone to occur. Its chief function therefore is to aid the primary zone in achieving a high combustion efficiency. Air is then added more rapidly in the dilution zone to reduce combustion temperatures to the level required by the turbine. It is added in such a way as to ensure that a good temperature-traverse quality is generated at the exit from the zone to prevent material problems in the turbine stage of the engine. The one remaining performance criterion discussed, that of durability, is satisfied by the addition of cooling strips to the walls of the combustor, which serve to direct a portion of the incoming cold air around these inner walls.

3.3 Effect of combustor design variables on pollutant formation

The concentration levels of most pollutant in Table 2 can be related directly to the temperature, time and concentration histories that exist in the combustor. These histories will vary, of course, from combustor to combustor and also with a change in operating conditions for any one combustor. Pollutant levels can only be quantified with precision in the light of such details, but an attempt will be made to relate different pollutant-species emissions qualitatively with the flow processes described previously.

Carbon monoxide

Carbon monoxide is formed at the flame front in concentrations that greatly exceed the equilibrium values, and is only oxidised further to the dioxide if it experiences an adequate temperature/time history to achieve this state. Equilibrium concentration levels at typical turbine entry conditions are effectively zero. The presence of carbon monoxide in gas-turbine exhausts therefore indicates either excessive generation due to inadequate mixing qualities in the primary zone, and/or too rapid cooling of the post-flame products that can arise as a result of quenching at the cooled walls, and/or by the too rapid cooling of the bulk flow by air addition to the intermediate or dilution zones. Clearly, poor fuel atomisation and poor air-flow distribution, such as excessive wall cooling and early addition of dilution air, both serve to increase carbon-monoxide levels, and high-temperature operation tends to reduce the level.

Hydrocarbons

Hydrocarbon pollutants may take the form of unburned fuel or thermally degraded products of the fuel. Such products include methane, the aldehydes, the acetylenes etc. Clearly, the same considerations apply to the degraded products as apply to carbon monoxide, but other factors must also be considered to account for the unburned fuel. The presence of the fuel indicates either that the fuel droplets formed in the combustor are too large to burn completely in the primary zone and/or that large volumes of the combustor operate at temperature much lower than the stoichiometric temperature.

Smoke (or carbon)

Smoke in gas turbine exhausts consists mostly of carbon. Carbon, like carbon monoxide, is produced in quantities in excess of the equilibrium concentrations, so the same considerations apply to smoke as to carbon monoxide. A significant variation in the kinetic behaviour of the two is that carbon is only formed at low pressures if the fuel/air ratio exceeds about 1·5 times the stoichiometric value. The effect of an increase in operating pressure becomes significant therefore for carbon formation, as burning limits widen with pressure. Fuel-rich regions that do not burn at low pressure will, for this reason alone, produce smoke at high pressures.

Sulphur dioxide

Sulphur is easily oxidised to the dioxide, and essentially all sulphur present in the fuel will exist as the dioxide in the exhaust gases.

Oxides of nitrogen

Most of the oxides of nitrogen emitted from gas turbines exist as nitric oxide NO, which is formed by the oxidation of atmospheric nitrogen and controlled by the concentrations of molecular and atomic levels of the nitrogen and oxygen species (Reference 13). For residence times typical of most gas-turbine combustors (approximately 10 ms), significant quantities of nitric oxide are only produced at temperatures in excess of 2000K. Such temperatures exist only in the primary zone, (or early intermediate zone); so factors that increase the temperature in this zone will also increase nitric oxide. Inlet temperature to the combustor, the fraction of fuel that burns near to the stoichiometric air/fuel ratio and the time spent at the high temperature level are the main factors to consider. The importance of equivalence ratio for a constant CIT is demonstrated in Table 5 below, which shows the very rapid rise in both

92

equilibrium concentration and rate of formation that accompanies the rise in
temperature caused by the change in equivalence ratio.

Table 5

Nitric-oxide formation characteristics

Φ_p	T_{Flame} deg R	NO_{Equil} parts in 10^6	NO_{Formed} parts in 10^6
0·6	3580	4740	1
0·8	4160	6820	536
1·0	4500	4520	1677
1·2	4450	864	273

$$\text{CIT} = 1300^{\circ}\text{R}$$
$$\text{P} = 5 \text{ atm}$$
$$\text{Residence time} = 3 \text{ ms}$$

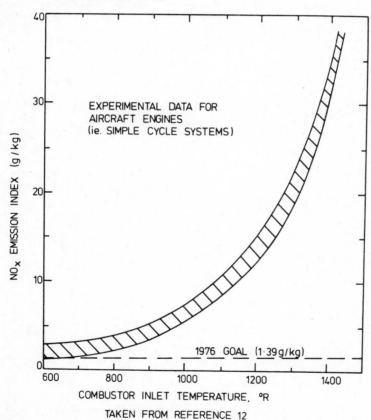

EXPERIMENTAL DATA FOR
AIRCRAFT ENGINES
(ie. SIMPLE CYCLE SYSTEMS)

1976 GOAL (1·39 g/kg)

NO$_X$ EMISSION INDEX (g/kg)

COMBUSTOR INLET TEMPERATURE, °R

TAKEN FROM REFERENCE 12

Fig. 9   Correlation of NO$_X$ emissions data with combustor inlet temperature

This dependence on temperature is also shown in Fig. 9, on which is plotted aircraft
gas-turbine engine data as a function of combustor-inlet temperature. Not all engine

data fall within the region shown, but it does include by far the greatest number of engines. The emission index in grams of NO_x per kilogram of fuel is observed to rise to nearly 40 at a combustor-inlet temperature of 1400°R, whereas the 1976 standard requires a level below 1·4 g/kg. But, as was shown in Section 2, the combustor-inlet temperature essentially controls the fuel-consumption characteristics for regenerative cycles, and, at 1400°R, the SFC for the gas turbine is not competitive with the piston engine. This temperature must be increased to at least 1750°R to achieve an acceptable SFC, hence significant modifications must be made to the design approach inherent in the aircraft gas-turbine combustor if the gas turbine is to be competitive in the automotive market.

3.4 Effect of part-power load conditions on pollutant formation

As a gas-turbine engine changes its operating condition from full power to idle, significant changes occur in the combustor performance conditions. These changes may conveniently be represented, for pollutant-emissions considerations, by the method shown in Fig. 10. This Figure demonstrates the changes in primary-zone operating conditions and the combustion loading parameter, a parameter that may be related directly to combustion efficiency, as the engine performance changes. At full power, the primary zone is shown to operate around the stoichiometric condition and at high efficiency, whereas, at idle, the zone operates at a lower temperature with a significantly lower combustion efficiency. Not shown directly by this performance map is the fact

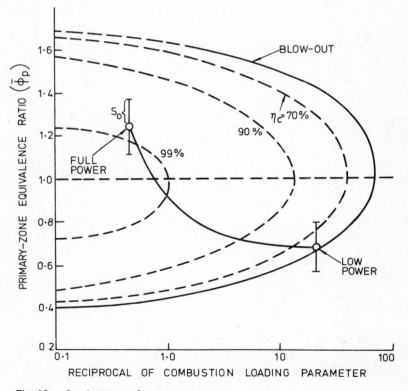

Fig. 10 Combustor performance map

94

that the combustor operating pressure also decreases with decreasing power output. From the considerations of Section 3.3, one can predict therefore the pollutant trends shown clearly in Table 4; i.e. at idle operation where the efficiency is low, large concentrations of hydrocarbons and carbon monoxide are formed, whereas, at the full-power level, when the primary zone is hotter at a relatively high pressure, nitric-oxide emissions and carbon production levels become dominant. Fig. 10 might lead one to believe that the emissions could be reduced if the temperature at idle were to be increased by increased equivalence ratio in the primary zone. This approach would reduce CO and HC, but it would result in high smoke emissions at high power output as the equivalence ratios would well exceed the stoichiometric condition.

3.5 Summary

The emissions of the pollutants of interest have been related to the combustor design and operating conditions. The high levels of CO and HC produced at low power level operation have been shown to be related to the low efficiency, low temperatures that must result if the primary zone is to operate at the stoichiometric condition during maximum power output operation. High levels of NO_x emissions have been related to the high combustor-inlet temperature for aircraft engine systems.

4 Pollutant reduction

Unfortunately, the process of combustor design today does not make it possible to relate quantitatively most of the performance requirements, e.g. combustion stability, ignitability, etc. to the combustor design and operating characteristics. Consequently, it is only possible to point to the directions required in design changes to reduce pollutant emissions, and the practical limit to which these directions can be pursued has to be determined experimentally.

There have been many experimental programmes reported in recent years in which the objective has been to reduce pollutant levels from gas-turbine engines in general, and automotive gas turbines in particular, but, as yet, no one has managed to achieve the goal set by the 1976 US Auto Standards (Table 4). Test results for simulated regenerative gas-turbine cycles have shown that HC and CO can be reduced drastically over the complete operating range to levels below the standard (Reference 7), but that NO_x levels remain about five times the goal level at the maximum-power level. As Fig. 9 shows, this already represents a large reduction in NO_x as current engine systems that operate at comparable combustor-inlet temperatures exhibit NO_x values nearly 30 times the goal level.

Further NO_x reductions are still feasible, however, and techniques by which this may be achieved will be discussed and quantified under two separate subheadings — for 'modified conventional combustors' and for 'advanced combustors'. This classification is somewhat arbitrary, but it is meant to imply that the latter method involves a greater change in design philosophy for the combustor designer.

4.1 Modified conventional combustors

The pollutant-emission levels discussed above for the simulated regenerative-cycle tests show a significant improvement over those that can be obtained from present-day aircraft engines. These levels reflect both the fact that the tests were made on a combustor designed for low emissions and the fact that the regenerative combustor operates at high temperatures and generally higher residence times than are found in the aircraft engine. Both factors improve HC and CO emission levels (Section 3.3), and, coupled with the low pressure level of operation, also reduce smoke emissions below visibility levels. It is these high temperature levels that promote the NO_x emissions, however, and the concentration of the specie must be reduced within the combustor if the gas turbine is to be used in automotive applications.

Before considering methods of NO_x reduction, it is worth while to study more closely the details of its formation characteristics in the conventional gas-turbine combustor. From previous considerations (Section 3.3), it is known that flame temperature and air-fuel concentrations greatly influence the rate of formation of NO_x and that the highest temperatures normally occur in the region of the primary zone. As the fuel is injected in the form of liquid droplets, it can be expected that the burning conditions are far from being homogeneous and that local hot spots will occur within the zone. The presence and size of these hot spots will clearly influence NO_x emissions considerably. This effect can be shown quantitatively by the method presented in Reference 13 and which has been verified experimentally for aircraft gas-turbine combustors. This method adopts a simple statistical approach to the flow processes in the combustor, and introduces a single parameter to define the state of inhomogeneity in the combustor. This is termed the 'mixedness' parameter, and is quantified in a dimensionless form as $S_0 = \sigma_0/\bar{\Phi}_p$, where σ_0 in statistical terms is called the standard deviation and represents the degree of distribution about the mass mean equivalence ratio in the primary zone $\bar{\Phi}_p$. Regions with equivalence ratios bounded between Φ and $\Phi + d\Phi$ are then represented by the mass fraction $f(\Phi) \, d\Phi$, where

$$f(\Phi) = (1/\sigma\sqrt{2\pi}) \exp\left[-(\Phi-\bar{\Phi}_p)^2/2\sigma^2\right]$$

This mixedness parameter is convenient to use, as the value $S_0 = 0$ corresponds to perfect mixing of the fuel and air prior to combustion and $S_0 = 1$ corresponds to a very poor mixing quality. Aircraft engine combustors have been shown to operate within the range $0 \cdot 3 - 0 \cdot 7$.

The influence of the quality of mixing S_0, and the mass mean primary zone equivalence ratio $\bar{\Phi}_p$, NO emissions are shown in Fig. 11. The results demonstrate that the emission index can vary from zero to 60 g/kg fuel for the same operating condition and that the design that favours low NO are low values of $\bar{\Phi}_p$ coupled with a very good quality of mixing. The NO_x emission goal corresponds to approximately 1·4 units in this Figure; hence it shows that the goal may be achieved with fuel and air equivalence ratios that are premixed before combustion and at values less than 0·8 stoichiometric, or, for example, with Φ_p at 0.5 and S_0 equal to 0·6. Very fuel-rich primary zones may also produce low NO_x, as shown by the Figure, but as typical overall combustor equivalence ratios are less than 0.3 stoichiometric, it is unlikely that this state can be attained without significant production of NO_x during the dilution process.

The results in Fig. 11 suggest methods that may be adopted to reduce NO_x and also show the sensitivity in the emission level to the two design parameters considered, $\bar{\Phi}_p$ and S_0. Premixed combustors offer the best solution it appears, and these are presently being pursued in the USA, but they will drastically modify the stability and ignitability of the systems developed. Whether these effects limit its application or not will only be decided experimentally. The approach in which the primary zone operates fuel-lean with a good mixing quality has been pursued (Reference 7), and is the basis for the comments made at the introduction to this section. It is limited, however, again by stability and ignitability criteria as it is not possible to operate with $\bar{\Phi}_p$ values at the level required to achieve the NO_x goal. This limitation may be overcome if a combustor is designed to operate with variable geometry, and this will be considered later.

Alternative methods of NO_x reduction in gas-turbine combustors may be employed that have the common object of reducing top temperatures in the combustor. Cooling tubes have been placed within the primary zone of experimental combustors (Reference 15), but their influence on HC and CO emission levels were not measured, and they are also unlikely to find application in the gas turbine. A more attractive

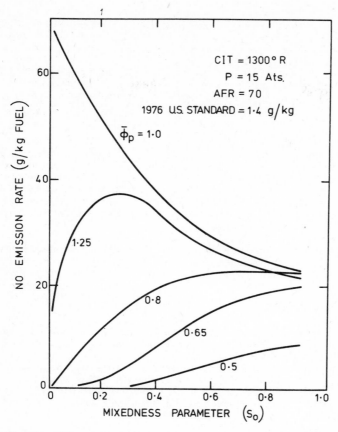

Fig. 11 Effects of fuel distribution on predicted NO emission rate

method employs the injection of water into the primary zone or into the compressor air prior to combustion (Reference 16), and experimental results show that equal mass flows of water and fuel reduce NO_x levels by approximately 50%. Current injection methods blanket the whole of the primary zone; but it is clear from the calculations presented above that significant improvements can be made in mass effectiveness if attention is paid only to the hot spots in the zone. A water supply is necessary for this method, of course; so it is likely that it will only find application in stationary gas-turbine systems.

4.2 Advanced combustors

Previous considerations clearly show that the most effective means of NO_x control involves a reduction in the primary-zone equivalence ratio $\bar{\Phi}_p$. There are severe limitations to the degree to which this can be achieved with the conventionally designed combustor, as an unavoidable consequence of the design is that the value of $\bar{\Phi}_p$ at idle levels reduces to about one-half the value at the point of maximum power. Combustion regions with fuel/air ratios at about one-half stoichiometric value are not stable, are prone to blow out, and usually operate at low combustion efficiencies. This behaviour, in fact, is responsible for the high carbon-monoxide and hydrocarbon emission levels that characterise today's gas-turbine engines. Clearly, a reduction in $\bar{\Phi}_p$ at design point

97

will only aggravate the situation at idle conditions, unless a design can be adopted that prevents this large reduction in $\bar{\Phi}_p$. It is also clear that any design that reduces $\bar{\Phi}_p$ at maximum power and increases $\bar{\Phi}_p$ at idle will simultaneously improve emission levels of all pollutant species currently under study. To achieve this in practice requires that either the fuel-distribution characteristics or the air-distribution characteristics are variable with changes in engine power level. The former is referred to as the staged-combustion concept, and the latter as the variable-geometry concept.

Staged combustion

This concept requires the combustor to operate with a small primary system, the products from which then serve as the pilot for one or more larger, secondary combustion zones downstream. The intention is that the small primary system would be designed to operate as far below the stoichiometric condition as can be achieved without violating the requirements of ignitability, stability and of the other performance criteria. The hot pilot gases would then permit the secondary zones to burn fuel at much lower stoichiometric conditions.

The mathematical model previously described has been used to confirm the potential of this concept, but only experimental testing will decide how low a value of NO_x can be achieved without significant sacrifice to the other performance characteristics.

Variable-geometry combustors

The purpose of the variable geometry would be to modify that fraction of air that enters the combustor primary zone as the engine operating conditions change. Maximum air fraction would enter at full power and minimum air fraction at idle, and, in this way, it is possible to design for a constant Φ_p over the full engine-operating range. The type of geometry envisaged is shown in Fig. 12, in which the airflow distribution is controlled by a movable valve. With such a design, it may be possible to operate certain gas-turbine systems with primary-zone equivalence ratios at 0·6 or less at maximum power output and so achieve the considerable NO_x reductions predicted in Fig. 11.

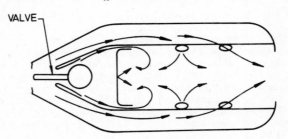

VARIABLE GEOMETRY COMBUSTOR

Fig. 12   Variable-geometry combustor

Variable-geometry combustors have recently been designed and tested as concept-proving studies (Reference 17) specifically for automobile-engine use. One combustor operated with a primary zone designed for a mass mean equivalence ratio of 0·5 over the full engine-operating range, and performed satisfactorily in terms of combustor stability, ignitability etc. At steady-state conditions, HC and smoke emissions were practically nonexistent, CO levels at idle were well below the desired level, but NO_x levels were approximately twice the goal figure (Table 6).

Table 6

Emission levels measured from a variable-geometry combustor

	NO_x	CO	HC
		g/kg fuel	
1976 US Federal Standards	1·39	11·8	1·5
Variable-geometry combustor* (Reference 17)	2·5	7·1	0

$$*\overline{\Phi}_p = 0\cdot5$$
$$CIT = 1300°R$$

These results represent the first results obtained from the combustor, and it is reasonable to expect that further development will reduce the NO_x level to the required standard.

5 Noise reduction

It is unlikely that any automotive gas turbine will ever operate at noise levels greater than that from piston engines, or that it will fail to satisfy any forseeable future legislation. The main sources of noise from aircraft gas-turbine engines, namely jet noise and fan noise in high bypass ratio fanjets, are not present in the engine cycle concepts considered. Further, its relatively high power/weight ratio will ensure that sufficient space is available and that the conventional sound-proofing materials may be used to surround the engine.

6 Conclusions

The following conclusions can be made about the automotive gas turbine:

(a) It is likely that engines in the 100-200 hp range will soon find application in the automobile, that they will employ a regenerative-free-power-turbine cycle, and that they will operate with a fuel consumption better than that for the present-day reciprocating engines.

(b) The use of new materials, such as the ceramics, can considerably reduce specific fuel consumption and increase specific power output.

(c) State-of-the-art combustor design is sufficient to reduce all pollutants except NO_x to levels below the 1976 US Federal Standards.

(d) Future studies of premixed-fuel systems for conventional combustors, and of advanced combustor concepts such as fuel-staging and variable geometry, are likely to reduce NO_x emissions to levels close to the standard level.

(e) The noise levels developed by such engines will not exceed any forseeable legislative standards.

7 Acknowledgements

I would like to acknowledge the support provided by K.W. Ramsden and Flt. Lt. D.J. Harris in the preparation of Section 2.

8 References

1 SHEPHERD, D.G.: 'Introduction to the gas turbine', (Whitefriars Press, 1960)

2 CARTER, A.F.: 'A 2000-hp military vehicle gas turbine — a study of significant thermodynamic and mechanical parameters'. ASME 68-GT-52, Washington, 1968

3 BALLAL, D.R. and LEFEBVRE, A.H.: 'A proposed method for calculating film — cooled wall temperatures in gas turbine combustors'. ASME Paper 72-WA/HT-24, New York, 1972

4 RAHKE, C.J.: 'The variable geometry power turbine'. SAE Paper 690031, 1969

5 JUDGE, A.W.: 'Small gas turbines' (MacMillan, 1960)

6 TURUNEN, W.A. and COLLMAN, J.G.: 'The General Motors Research GT-309 gas turbine engine', SAE Trans., 1966, 74, Paper 650714

7 CORNELIUS, W., STIVENDER, D.L., and SULLIVAN, R.E.: 'A combustion system for a vehicle regenerative gas turbine featuring low air pollutant emissions'. SAE Progress in Technology, Vol. 14, Paper 670936

8 AYRES, R.U., and RENNER, R.: 'Automotive emission control: alternatives to the internal combustion engine'. 5th APCA West Coast, tech. meeting, San Francisco, October 1970

9 WRIGHT, E.S., GREENWALD, L.E. and DAVISON, W.R.: 'Manufacturing cost study of selected gas turbine autombile engine concepts'. Report PB-202251 NTIS, Department of Commerce, Springfield, Va. 22151, USA

10 RESTALL, J.E.: 'An examination of some ceramic materials for high temperature gas turbine engines'. First international symposium on air-breathing engines, Marseille, June 1972

11 FARMER, R.C.: 'Where are the ceramic turbines?' gas-turbine international, July 1972

12 SAWYER, R.F.: 'Atmosphere pollution by aircraft engines and fuels'. AGARD-AR-40, March 1972

13 FLETCHER, R.S., and HEYWOOD, J.B.: 'A model for nitric oxide emissions from aircraft gas turbine engines'. Paper 71-123, 9th AIAA aerospace sciences meeting, New York, January 1971

14 FLETCHER, R.S., SIEGEL, R.D. and BISTRESS, E.K.: 'The control of oxide of nitrogen emissions from aircraft gas turbine engines'. NREC Report 1162-1, Northern Research & Engineering Corporation, Cambridge, Mass., USA, December 1971

15 HAZARD, H.R.: 'NO_x emissions from experimental compact combustors'. ASME 72-GT-108, San Francisco, March 1972

16 HILT, M.B. and JOHNSON, R.H.: 'Nitric oxide abatement in heavy duty gas turbine combustors by means of aerodynamics and water injection', ASME 72-GI-53, San Francisco, March 1972

17 DEMETRI, E.P., et al.: 'Low NO_x combustor study Northern Research Engineering, Corporation, Cambridge, Mass. USA, EPA Contract 68-04-0017

8 The Stirling engine

G. Rice, B.Sc., Ph.D., C.Eng., M.I.Mech.E.
Lecturer in Engineering Science, University of Reading, England

1 Introduction

Conversion of energy at poor thermal efficiency is relatively easy and inexpensive to achieve. There is, however, a need for increased attention to conservation of resources. The majority of energy conversion is achieved by heat engines, and the Rankine steam cycle is dominant. The internal-combustion engine is used almost exclusively for automotive use. The gas turbine (Joule cycle) is becoming competitive with the Diesel engine in the intermediate power range (i.e. below that at which the steam cycle is at present practical). These existing systems become inefficient at low powers. Exhaust emission from internal-combustion engines presents major problems of pollution. Legislative requirements in the USA, particularly, are forcing manufacturers of these engines to pay considerable attention to this problem. Environmentalists are also concerned with noise and vibration levels of devices, and once again the internal-combustion engines, especially the diesel, are major offenders. A closed-cycle energy-conversion system is, however, inherently quiet, and the external-combustion process being continuous results in low pollutant level of exhaust products. A modern contender of the closed-cycle systems is the Stirling engine. The cycle itself is not new, and was patented by Robert Stirling in 1816 (Reference 1), but advances in materials technology within this century have led to developments possibly unimaginable 100 years ago.

The Stirling engine is a heat engine — according to the classical definition that heat is supplied from a reservoir at high temperature and heat is rejected at a lower temperature with the difference being available as work output, as illustrated by Fig. 1. In all true heat engines, the conversion device works according to a cycle, and the working fluid is contained within a closed system or boundary. The Stirling engine has a gas as the working fluid, and the specific output is a function of the mass and pressure of the charge. The materials of construction available to Robert Stirling in the 19th century considerably impeded the early developments of the machine, and the low working pressures attainable allowed for very low specific output even compared with early steam-generating plant. Towards the end of Robert Stirling's life, in 1876, he gave this account of the problem: 'These imperfections have been in a great measure removed by time and especially by the genius of the distinguished Bessemer. If Bessemer iron and steel had been known 35 or 40 years ago, there is scarce a doubt that the air engine would have been a great success. It remains for some skilled and ambitious mechanist in a future age to repeat it under more favourable circumstances and with complete success (Reference 1). Some hundred years on, we are now in the fortunate position to ask: Was Robert Stirling right in his prediction? Indeed, have the favourable circumstances been reached, and with what success? To answer this question, we have to start at the point in time where 20th-century materials and fabrication techniques were applied to the problem. The real advance started in 1938, when the Philips Company considered the Stirling engine as a possible solution for providing power supplies for radio receivers and transmitters (Reference 2). Work continued through the Second World War, and the Philips results aroused considerable interest in the US Navy specially, at the end of the war. The advent of the transistor eliminated the need for such power supplies, and Philips turned attention to the design of larger engines. The early engines were air-charged to about 10 atm pressure, but the later high-powered engines were charged with either helium or hydrogen to above 100 atm (Reference 3).

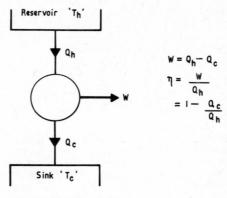

$$W = Q_h - Q_c$$
$$\eta = \frac{W}{Q_h}$$
$$= 1 - \frac{Q_c}{Q_h}$$

Fig. 1   Heat Engine

For the Stirling engine to compete in specific power output ratings, with say, the diesel engine, it must operate at high pressure ($>$ 100 atm) with helium or hydrogen as the working fluid. The operating temperature must exceed 600°C to attain efficiencies comparable with that obtainable with the modern high-speed diesel. These requirements, taken together, produce a formidable problem in design — even with modern materials and fabrication techniques. Even if we are in a position to meet the necessary engineering demands, the question may still be asked: Why the Stirling engine? To attempt an answer requires a detailed understanding of the problem in design and manufacture of the device, the characteristics of its performance, and an estimate of its cost in mass production.

2   The Stirling-engine cycle

The cycle is best illustrated by reference to pressure/volume and temperature/entropy plots (Fig. 2).

Compression occurs in a 'cold space' by the action of a working piston, and the gas is then transferred to a 'hot space' — via a regenerator by the action of a second piston, referred to as the displacer (displacement piston). Expansion then occurs, with the working fluid ideally wholly contained within the heated space, by simultaneous movement of the displacement and working pistons. The fluid is finally returned to the cold side of the engine by movement of the displacement piston — to complete the cycle. In the ideal cycle, the fluid is compressed isothermally (process $1 - 2$), regeneration occurs at constant volume ($2 - 3$), followed by isothermal expansion ($3 - 4$), and finally constant-volume regeneration ($4 - 1$). After compression ($1 - 2$) at temperature T_c, say, the gas is heated 'internally' by the regenerator to the temperature of the hot space (or reservoir), T_h. After expansion ($3 - 4$) at temperature T_h, the gas is cooled 'internally' by the regenerator to the temperature of the cold space, T_c. The regenerator is seen to act as a thermal-storage device, and the negative and positive energy transfers during the constant-volume processes $2 - 3$ and $4 - 1$, respectively, are equal, thus resulting in no exchange of heat with the surroundings in varying the temperature of the fluid. In the ideal cycle, the following simple thermodynamic analysis applies.

102

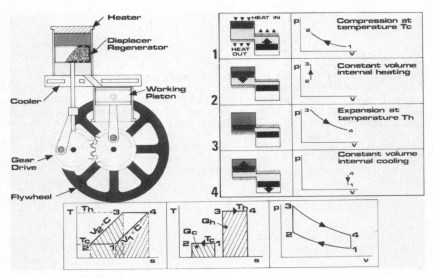

Fig. 2 Stirling engine cycle

Work done during compression $W_{1-2} = -m\,RT_c \ln r_v$ (1)

Heat exchange, between gas
and regenerator $Q_{2-3} = m\,C_v(T_h - T_c)$ (2)

Work done during expansion $W_{3-4} = m\,RT_h \ln r_v$ (3)

Heat exchange between gas
and regenerator $Q_{4-1} = -m\,C_v\,(T_h - T_c)$ (4)

Thermal efficiency θ = $\dfrac{W}{\text{heat supplied}}$ (5)

Heat supplied $= Q_{3-4}$ $(\because Q_{2-3} = -\,Q_{4-1})$ (6)

and, from the first law of thermodynamics:

$$Q_{1-2} - W_{1-2} = 0$$

$$Q_{3-4} - W_{3-4} = 0$$

for an isothermal process, and $W = m\,RT \ln^r v$ for a closed system.

Thus θ = $\dfrac{W_{1-2} + W_{3-4}}{W_{3-4}}$ - $\dfrac{(T_h - T_c)\,mR\ln^r v}{m\,R\,T_h \,\ln r_v}$ (7)

          = $\dfrac{1 - T_c}{T_h}$

which is equal to the Carnot efficiency.

Note that   m = mass of working gas

R = gas constant

r_v = volume ratio v_1/v_2.

The above analysis is for zero regenerator volume. The regenerator must, of course, have sufficient mass and volume to store the energy equivalent to $Q_{2\text{-}3}$ and $Q_{4\text{-}1}$ with negligible variation in local temperatures during the exchange processes. This volume will cause a reduction in specific output but cause no reduction in efficiency, provided that the processes are reversible. The cycle is reversible and the system may be operated as an engine, refrigerator or heat pump (Fig.3). To accomplish the ideal cycle, it may be noted that the movement of the respective pistons would need to take place in a discontinuous fashion. The work output for discontinuous motion of the pistons, allowing for the ideal cycle to prevail, but with volume of the regenerator V_R, is given by

$$W = mR (T_c \ln P_1/P_2 + T_h \ln P_3/P_4) \qquad (8)$$

where $$\frac{P_1}{P_2} = \frac{V_2 T_R + V_R (T_c - T_R)}{V_1 T_R + V_R (T_c - T_R)} \qquad (9)$$

and $$\frac{P_3}{P_4} = \frac{V_1 T_R + V_R (T_h - T_R)}{V_2 T_R + V_R (T_h - T_R)} \qquad (10)$$

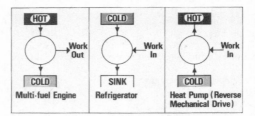

Fig. 3   Modes of operation

Discontinuous motion of the pistons is impractical, and it is usual to accept sinusoidal movement of the pistons with their phasing arranged to approximate to the ideal cycle. The volume variation in the 'cold space' (V_1) and 'hot space' (V_2) for a typical engine is illustrated in Fig. 4. Comparison is made with ideal discontinuous motion of the pistons. The phase angle between the pistons is usually about 90°, but the precise value depends on the geometry of the engine and the volume ratios of the 'cold space', 'hot space', regenerator etc. The shape of the pressure-volume diagram resulting from sinusoidal motion is shown in Fig. 5. Generalised thermodynamic analysis of the cycle and optimisation of phase angle have been undertaken by Finkelstein (References 4 and 5).

3   Engine geometry

There exists three basic configurations of engine layout, and these have been classified as a, β and γ (Fig. 6). The a type has two separate cylinders, cold and hot sides of the engine, each with a working piston. The β has one cylinder with two pistons, one of which is the working piston and the other is a displacer. The γ engine has two cylinders with a working piston in the cooled cylinder and a displacer piston within the heated cylinder . In the β and γ engines, the regenerator may be fixed or may be integral with the displacer, and the alternatives are illustrated for the β and γ types, respectively, in Fig. 6.

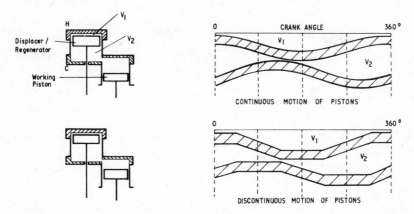

Fig. 4   Volume variation for gamma-type engine

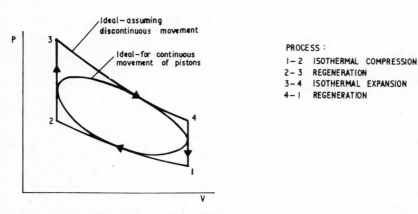

Fig. 5   Pressure/volume diagram of Stirling engine

PROCESS :

1 – 2   ISOTHERMAL COMPRESSION
2 – 3   REGENERATION
3 – 4   ISOTHERMAL EXPANSION
4 – 1   REGENERATION

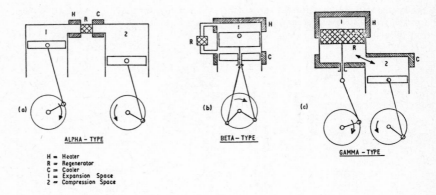

Fig. 6   Main types of Stirling engine

The a and γ engines suffer in terms of power output, compared with the β engine, because of partial transfer of gas through the regenerator during the expansion stroke (Fig. 7). A further disadvantage suffered by the a engine, compared with both β and γ types, is the fact that one of the working pistons has to seal on the hot side of the engine. In the β and γ engines, the working piston only has to be sealed to atmosphere, and this side of the engine is cooled.

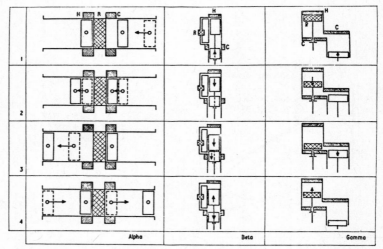

Fig. 7   Sequence of operation of alpha, beta and gamma-type engines in discontinuous motion

4   Drive arrangements

Numerous crank and gear drive mechanisms exist for each of the engine geometries, possibly the simplest being that illustrated by Fig. 2. Perhaps the most well known, and in many ways unique, mechanism applied to the Stirling engine is the Rhombic drive developed by Philips (References 3 and 6); see Figs. 8 and 9. The mechanism allows for complete dynamic balance of the machine while providing excellent phasing of the pistons. Philips have allied this design to their patented 'Roll-sock' seal (Reference 7).

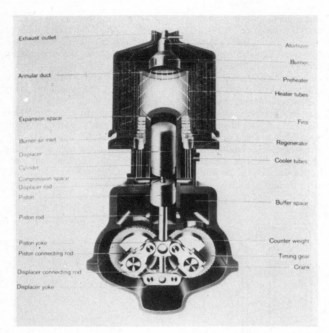

Exhaust outlet
Annular duct
Expansion space
Burner air inlet
Displacer
Cylinder
Compression space
Displacer rod
Piston
Piston rod
Piston yoke
Piston connecting rod
Displacer connecting rod
Displacer yoke

Atomizer
Burner
Preheater
Heater tubes
Fins
Regenerator
Cooler tubes
Buffer space
Counter weight
Timing gear
Crank

Fig. 8 Section through single-cylinder Stirling engine with rhombic drive

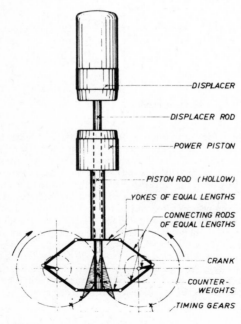

DISPLACER
DISPLACER ROD
POWER PISTON
PISTON ROD (HOLLOW)
YOKES OF EQUAL LENGTHS
CONNECTING RODS OF EQUAL LENGTHS
CRANK
COUNTER-WEIGHTS
TIMING GEARS

Fig. 9 Rhombic drive

107

Sealing presents a major problem, and a possible solution proposed by P.D. Dunn et al. (Reference 8) is illustrated in Fig. 10. The engine is of the β type, and the working piston consists of a 'hydraulic bag' that is sealed to both the cylinder and the displacement piston. The arrangement shown in Fig. 10 shows the displacement piston being hydraulically actuated by a swash plate. The swash plate is driven by the hydrostatic pressure exerted on the hydraulic-bag working piston of the engine. The cycle and mode of operation of the system is illustrated by Fig. 11. The power output of the engine is varied by variation in angle of the swash plate. The double acting Stirling engine proposed by Rinia (References 9 and 10) provides a unique solution for multicylinder operation with use of a conventional crankshaft drive. In this configuration, each cylinder has a single piston with the underside (drive side) connected to the cold side of a regenerator for gas passage to the upperside of an adjacent cylinder, which is heated (Fig. 12). The adjacent pistons are 90° out of phase with one another. The major disadvantage of this design is the need to effect a reliable piston seal that is acting within a heated cylinder. The requirements for a displacer piston seal are much less stringent.

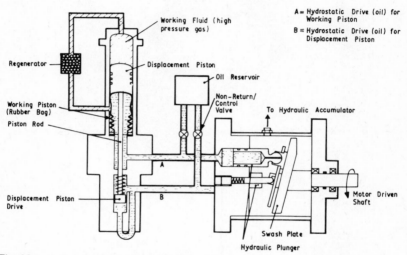

Fig. 10   Hydraulic fluid-drive Stirling engine

The free-piston Stirling engine developed by Beale (Reference 11) has the advantage of being hermetically sealed, since its moving parts require no external linkages. The geometry is of the β type, and the displacer and working pistons are connected to a buffer volume within the envelope of the system but sealed from the working space. The gas pressure within the working space of the engine varies with respect to the pressure in the buffer volume in such a way that the differing masses of the displacement and working pistons move out of phase with one another. There is a net reaction between the moving pistons and the containment vessel to cause the system to vibrate at a certain natural frequency. The device has been successfully demonstrated as a means for activating the plunger of a pump. Various possible configurations have been proposed by Beale (Reference 11), including that of a linear alternator. Rotary-engine geometries of the Wankel type have also been considered. The basic disadvantage of many of these proposals, in which one rotor acts as a compressor and the other as a displacer, is the need to operate the displacer rotor under high-temperature conditions.

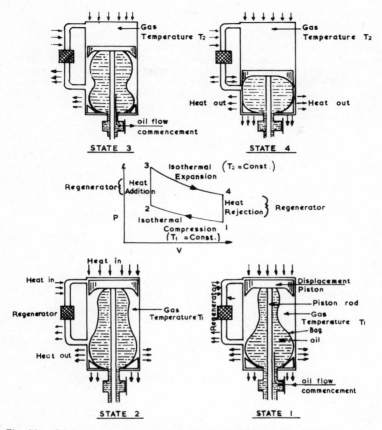

Fig. 11   Stirling engine - gas cycle (with liquid displacement fluid)

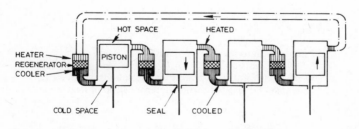

Fig. 12   Multi-cylinder double-acting Stirling engine

5   Regenerator

The regenerator is a thermal reservoir, and is inserted between the compression and expansion spaces of the engine to absorb heat from, and reject heat to, the gas that is transferred in an alternating manner between these two spaces. Regenerators are usually composed of a bed of finely divided materials, in the form of wire mesh, steel balls, metal wool, or ceramic particles, or sintered porous structure through which the gaseous working fluid can pass. The regenerator must be of sufficient capacity to provide the necessary internal heat transfer with minimum temperature variation of its structure.

$$Q_R = Q_{2\text{-}3} = Q_{4\text{-}1} = m_R \, C_{PR}, \, \Delta\theta$$

where m_R = mass of the regenerator

C_{PR} = specific heat of materials of construction

$\Delta\theta$ = temperature variation during energy transfer.

To effect heat transfer, there must be a temperature difference between the regenerator matrix and the gas. Therefore

$$Q_R = h \, \gamma \, s \, \Delta T$$

where h = heat transfer coefficient

s = surface area of the regenerator matrix

ΔT = local temperature difference between the regenerator matrix and the gas

γ = period of heat transfer (for process 2-3 or 4-1).

It is apparent from the above simple equations, 11 and 12, that the larger the mass and surface area of the regenerator the smaller will be the values $\Delta\theta$ and ΔT. A large regenerator volume, and hence mass of material, will, however, result in a reduction of specific output of the engine. Large surface area is provided by having small particles for construction of the matrix. Regenerator effectiveness E is defined as the ratio of the actual heat transferred to the heat that may ideally be transferred. The following approximate equation for the effectiveness may be considered:

$$E = \frac{(T_h - T_c) - n \, \Delta T}{(T_h - T_c)}$$

where n = constant.

It is seen that ΔT has to be zero for 100% effectiveness.

A detailed analysis of regenerator performance has been undertaken by Zarinchang (Reference 12), and, apart from experimental determination of heat transfer under sinusoidal flux conditions, he has analysed the variation of coefficient of performance for varying aspect ratio of the regenerator. He shows that effectiveness is increased with increase in the length/diameter ratio. This is due to the increased heat-transfer coefficient attainable at increased velocity. It is also seen that effectiveness is increased with reduction in molecular weight of the working gas. The length/diameter ratio with air as the working fluid is considerably restricted, compared with that attainable with helium or hydrogen, because of increased pressure drop.

Optimisation of the regenerator design involves minimising the pressure drop, due to flow of gas through the matrix, and providing the maximum surface area for heat transfer while attempting to maximise the regenerator effectiveness and minimise conduction losses. Both the latter are achieved by increasing the length/diameter ratio of the regenerator. The thermal efficiency of the engine can be written as

$$\frac{W_{net}}{Q + C_v (T_h - T_c) (1 - E) + Q_c}$$

where Q_c = conduction loss through the regenerator.

The net work output W_{net} is reduced with increased pressure drop. Complete analysis of performance under engine operating conditions is complex due to the cyclic nature of gas flow through the regenerator. The pressure drop causes holdup of fluid flow, and results in varying rates of flow between entry and exit of the regenerator at any instant.

6   Heat-exchanger design

Heat has to be transferred to and from the engine during separate and partly overlapping periods of the cycle. For continuous external combustion, the heat exchanger of the engine has to have sufficient thermal capacity to provide a uniform temperature within the expansion space. This usually presents no difficulties because of the pressure-vessel structural requirements of the heat exchanger. The compression side of the engine is usually water-cooled, and this part of the engine presents perhaps the least problem in design.

The high-temperature heat exchanger, designed to transfer heat at up to 800°C, presents a major design problem, since it has to withstand internal pressures perhaps as high as 200 atm. With the use of helium or hydrogen as working fluids, it becomes evident in the design of the heat exchanger, for transferring heat from the flame of a burner, that the geometry and surface-area requirement are set by the heat-transfer rates attainable by the combustion gases and not the charge fluid. The design of the Philips heat exchanger is illustrated in Fig. 13.

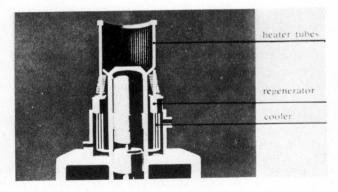

Fig. 13   Tubular Stirling engine heat-exchanger design

The exchanger is of tubular construction, and the major consideration in its design would be the provision of maximum area for heat transfer, on the combustion gas side, while ensuring minimum pressure drop and minimum volume within the engine.

Attention has recently turned to the application of heat pipes in allowing for simplification of the heat-exchanger construction while attaining improvement in heating rates resulting in reduced volume of the exchanger. A heat pipe is a device that effects an isothermal transfer of heat, and simply consists of a sealed tube, or other geometrical vessel, containing a liquid that is vaporised at one end and condensed at the other (Reference 13). Liquid is returned from the condenser to the evaporator by a 'wick', and it is this feature alone that distinguishes it from a thermal syphon (Fig. 14). The wick allows for transfer of fluid against gravity, and has the further advantage of enhancing both the evaporation and condensation rates of heat transfer. A system being developed at the Applied Physical Sciences Department, Reading University, is illustrated by Fig. 15, in which the condenser end of a sodium-charged heat pipe is integral with the heat exchanger of the engine, and the sodium vapour transfers heat from a fluidised-bed combustor. Performance measurements indicate a considerable improvement in heat-transfer rates within a fluidised-bed combustor, compared with a conventional flame exchanger. It has been showh that it is possible to obtain the equivalent heat-transfer rates with a fluidised-bed temperature of $950^{\circ}C$ as a flame at $2500^{\circ}C$ — for transfer to a body at $650^{\circ}C$. This considerable reduction in temperature of combustion leads to a reduction in the production of NO_x while further allowing for increased residence time and consequent reduction in otherwise unreacted hydrocarbons. The problems encountered in design of the heat exchanger are associated with irreversibilities. The geometry required for high heat-transfer rates leads inevitably to pressure losses. A detailed analysis of the problem has been presented by Creswick (Reference 14). He produces an equation for the flow area of the exchanger in terms of non-dimensional numbers — related to heat transfer, pressure drop and properties of the working fluid. The advantages of use of low-molecular-weight fluids become obvious for high speeds.

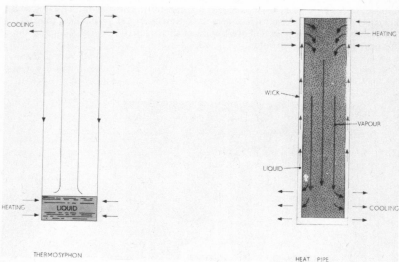

Fig. 14

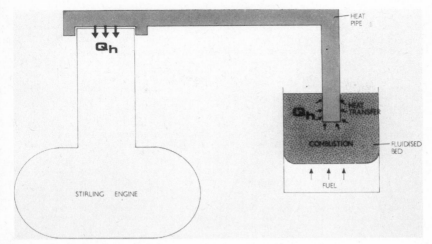

Fig. 15   Application of fluidised bed and heat pipe to Stirling engine

7   Engine characteristics

It has been established that a Stirling engine needs to be charged at high pressure
($\sim$ 100 atm) to develop specific power comparable to that of the modern/diesel
engine. There is, however, a considerable difference in the cyclic variation of pressure
for these devices (Fig. 16). The less rapid pressure variation with the Stirling engine
leads to a comparable reduction in structure-borne noise; see Fig. 17 (Reference 15).

Many of the characteristics of the Stirling engine have been published by Philips
(References 7 and 15), and reference to data for a hydrogen-charged engine (Fig. 18)
shows the effect of varying charge pressure with specific power on the engine
efficiency. The efficiency of energy conversion will, of course, also depend on the
performance of the combustion system and, in particular, the effectiveness of the
recuperator – which preheats air to the burner. Fig. 19 illustrates the proportion
of heat transferred to the engine Q_h to that which is required to be transferred from
the combustion gases to the air supplied to the burner Q_o. The overall efficiency of
conversion is given by

$$\eta o \quad = \quad \frac{\eta b \, \eta (1 - \mu)}{1 - X_R \mu}$$

where ηb =   burner efficiency

   η =   engine-cycle efficiency

   X_R =   recuperator effectiveness

   μ =   ratio of heat transferred in the recuperator to heat
            transferred to the engine (Q_o/Q_h; see Fig. 19)

It may be noted from this equation that the overall efficiency is very susceptible to
the value of μ. For a low combustion temperature and a corresponding large value of
μ, the overall conversion efficiency can be low even for a relatively high value of X_R.
The variation in performance with charge gas is illustrated by the plots of overall
efficiency and torque, against speed, given in Fig. 20 for air, helium and hydrogen.
It is important to notice, from the torque characteristic, that, at low speed, an
air-charged engine is comparable in performance to the helium and hydrogen-charged
engine. Viscous losses are dominant at high speed, and are reduced by use of low
molecular weight fluids, whereas, at low speed, leakage losses become significant and

the use of high molecular weight fluids is preferred. The efficiency and torque characteristics for varying charge pressure are indicated by Fig. 21.

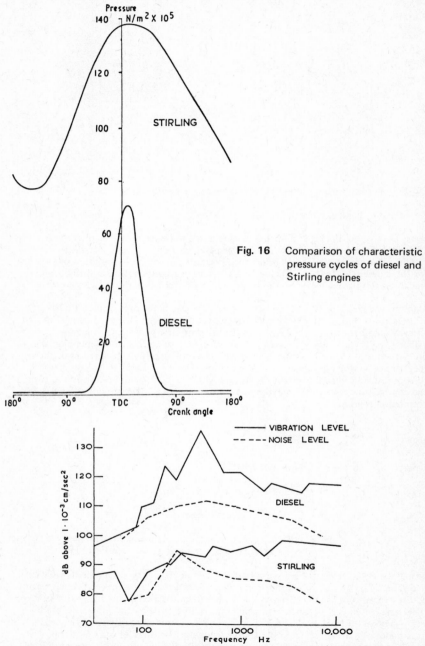

Fig. 16   Comparison of characteristic pressure cycles of diesel and Stirling engines

Fig. 17   Vibration and noise levels of 4-cylinder Stirling engine, compared with those of a diesel engine with the same output

114

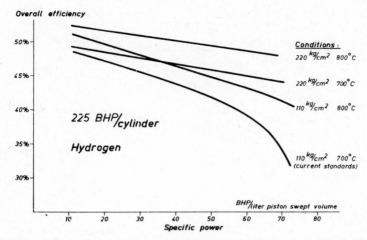

Fig. 18   Effect of mean pressure and heater temperature on optimal efficiency

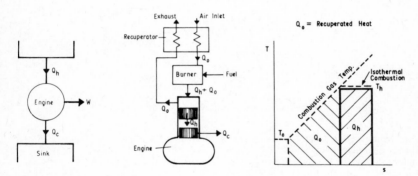

Fig. 19   Recuperation

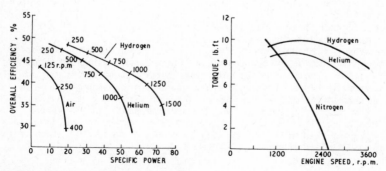

Fig. 20   Efficiency and torque variation

115

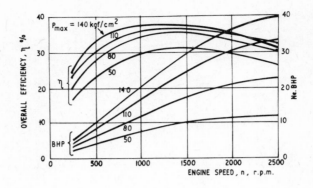

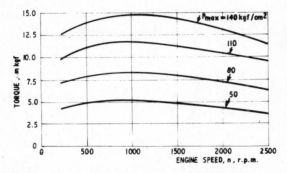

Fig. 21   Efficiency and torque variation with charge pressure

The Stirling engine accepts heat at relatively low temperatures (<750°C), and analysis of the heat balance will show that the proportion of heat supplied that is released to cooling is given by $(1 - \eta)\ Q_h$. The comparison in cooling requirement of the Stirling engine to the diesel engine is given in Fig. 22.

8   Pollution

The Stirling engine utilises an external continuous-combustion process that is readily controlled or preset for air/fuel ratio and optimum-combustion conditions. It is useful to compare the emission from the exhaust of such a burner with those from an internal-combustion engine. United Stirling (Sweden) A.B. & Co. has published a table showing the comparison of CO, NO and unburned hydrocarbons (Table 1). Considerable difficulties are being encountered in developing simple techniques for modifying the internal-combustion engine to meet current and future legislative requirements of the USA. Table 2 gives a comparison of the Stirling engine with internal-combustion engines with respect to the US Federal test requirements for 1976. The data for the internal-combustion engines was extracted from papers submitted at a conference on 'Air-pollution control in transport engines' (Reference 16). The quantity of HC and NO in g/mile is obtained by interpolation for an engine required for a vehicle of about 3000 lb weight.

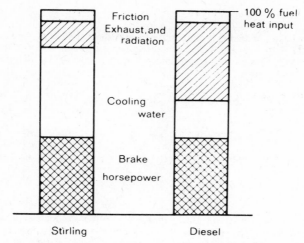

Fig. 22 Heat balances for Stirling and diesel engines

Table 1

Exhaust component	Stirling engine (diesel fuel)	Spark-ignition engine nonmodified (petrol)	Spark-ignition engine, modified* (petrol)	Spark-ignition engine (LPG)	Compression-ignition (diesel engine)	Regenerative gas turbine †
Carbon monoxide, (% vol.)	0·007–0·03	4 − 10	1·0 (max)	2 − 5	0·02 − 0·5	0·025 − 0·045
Unburned hydrocarbons parts in 10^6	1 − 2	500 − 2000	180 (max)	300−1500	200 − 4000	1 − 2
Nitric oxides parts in 10^6	100 − 200	600 − 2000	600−2000	800−2000	400 − 2000	90 − 250

* Modified to US Federal Specifications (1970)
related to a standardised driving cycle

† It should be noticed that the exhaust flow per
unit of energy of a gas turbine is more than four
times that of a Stirling or diesel engine.

Table 2

Considerable difficulties are being encountered in the development of the internal-combustion engine to meet the United States legislative requirements. Table 2 gives a comparison of the Stirling engine with internal-combustion engines with respect to the US Federal and California tests.

	Stirling engine	SI engine	CI engine	Gas turbine	1976 federal limit
CO, %	0·007 – 0·03	1·0 – 9·0	0·02 – 0·5	0·025 – 0·045	0·2
HC, g/mile	0·01 – 0·02	1·1 – 7·0	1·0 – 5·0	0·04 – 0·08	0·41
NO, g/mile	1·0 – 2·0	1·1 – 4·0	2·0 – 10·0	2·0 – 5·0	0·4

It is seen from Tables 1 and 2 that the Stirling engine offers a reduction in exhaust pollution. Considerable effort is being put into developments for improving emission levels of the internal-combustion engine, but, in general, they involve increased fuel consumption, weight and cost. Time appears to be a major factor in the development of an acceptable system in meeting the legislative requirements of the USA. It would appear to be impossible with the present rate of development of the Stirling engine to offer it as a large-scale alternative to the internal-combustion engine for automobile use within the next decade. The gas turbine is receiving considerable attention, and the major problem with the exhaust is seen from Tables 1 and 2 to be nitric oxide, which is aggravated by excess air. It is with regard to NO_x that most energy-conversion systems appear to be outside the required legislative limits. The major requirement for reduction in NO_x is a reduction in combustion temperature. Results of recent work on fluidised-bed combustion at the Applied Physical Sciences Department of Reading University indicate that the NO_x level is less than 50 parts in 10^6 at a combustion temperature of about 950°C (Reference 17). This would be within the 1976 US Federal limit.

9   Applications

The Stirling engine has the advantage of being able to maintain high efficiency for small power outputs. Power from a few watts to several hundred watts are required for communication and navigational purposes. These applications include flashing lights for navigational buoys, telecommunication, repeater stations and automatic weather stations. The major requirements for such devices are: reliability, long unattended life, no maintenance. Both radioisotope and fossil fuels may be used to power these generators.

In the range 1 kW – 20 kW, the Stirling engine would need to compete with existing internal combustion engines. A general requirement in many developing countries is the provision of pumping power. Dung-generated methane is readily obtainable. What is required is a simple, cheap, reliable engine. The only parameter that is of concern at present in covering these requirements by the Stirling engine is cost. The low-pressure air-charged engine is a possibility, and is suitable for local manufacture and maintenance.

Numerous agricultural and industrial applications exist for the engine. Stacker trucks using liquid or gaseous hydrocarbon fuel or thermal storage to heat the engine is an attractive application. Small boats may also be powered by the engine – using liquid or gaseous hydrocarbons. The multifuel capability and sealed-unit characteristics are advantageous, and the principal selling points will be absence of noise and vibration.

118

Portable generator sets may also benefit from the use of the Stirling engine. For the larger power requirements, 20 − 30 kW, the engine may become competitive with the diesel for buses and lorries.

10 Limitations and current developments

The Stirling engine suffers a major disadvantage compared with the internal-combustion engine for automotive use with regard to startup time. The time required to heat the engine to its operating temperature depends on the thermal capacity of the heat exchanger. With the basic requirement of having to withstand high pressures and temperature, there is considerable difficulty in reducing the mass of the exchanger. With the Philips heat exchanger, startup time is claimed to be as low as 15 s. Dynamic control may be affected by variation of the charge pressure, which involves a secondary reservoir and compressor for the use of helium or hydrogen, variation of phase angle of the pistons or variation of the volume. The latter method is readily achieved by use of the hydraulic fluid drive illustrated in Fig. 10. The engine requires almost a perfect seal when helium or hydrogen are used as working fluids. Gas buffering is a solution that has not appealed to the Philips Company, whose 'roll-sock' seal has proved to be very successful under long-life engine test conditions (7). The hydraulic-bag piston seal, as shown by Fig. 10 and 11, may also prove to be a solution to the problem.

Combustion and heat-exchanger design falls into two categories: pollution and the cost. Continuous combustion should imply good emission characteristics. Heat exchange, for transfer of heat from a flame, involves a complex design, which is likely to be an expensive feature of the engine. The integral heat-pipe/fluidised-bed system, outlined above, may overcome this deficiency. The fluidised bed introduces, however, a further source of thermal capacity to be accounted for at startup.

The major organisations involved with work on the Stirling engine for development of a commercial unit have been Philips (Holland), General Motors (USA), United Stirling (Sweden), MAN (Germany), and recently Ford of America. The factors which have not yet been satisfactorily cleared are the cost and specific power. The cost must be related to mass production, and predicted costs range from 1½ to 2 times that of an equivalent rated modern diesel engine.

11 References

1	ZARINCHANG, J.	'The Stirling engine − bibliography'. Intermediate Technology Development Group, London, 1972.
2	RINIA, H. and DU PRE, F.K.	'Air-engines', Philips Tech. Rev., 1946, **8**, (5).
3	MEIJER, R.J.	'Philips Stirling thermal engine', Philips Res. Rep., Suppl. 1961.
4	FINKELSTEIN, T.	'Generalised thermodynamic analysis of Stirling engines'. SAE Paper 118B, January 1960.
5	FINKELSTEIN, T.	'Optimization of phase angle and volume ratio for Stirling engines', SAE Paper 118C, January 1960.
6	VAN WEENAN, F.L.	'The construction of the Philips air engine', Philips Tech. Rev. **9**, (5), pp. 135-160 1947.

7	MEIJER, R.F.	'The Philips Stirling engine', Ingenieur, 1969, **81**, (18/19), 2nd May, pp.69-79; 9th May pp. 81-93.
8	DUNN, P.D. RICE, G. and MORGAN, K.E.	'Heat engines', UK Patent 3551/71
9	RINIA, H.	'New possibilities for the air engine'. Proc. Kon. Ned. Akad. Wet., **49**, 150-155 1946
10	VAN WEENEN, F.L.	'The construction of the Philips air engine', Philips Tech. Rev. 1947, **9**, (5), pp. 125-134.
11	BEALE, W.T.	'Free piston Stirling engines — model tests and simulations', International automotive-engineering congress, Detroit, Mich., January 1969.
12	ZARINCHANG, J.	'An investigation of some theoretical and experimental aspects of the stirling engine'., Ph.D. thesis, department of Applied Physical Sciences, Reading University, 1972.
13	GROVER, G.M., COTTER, T.P. and ERIKSON, G.F.	'Structures of very high thermal conductance', J. Appl. Phys. 1964 **35**, (6), pp.1990-1991.
14	CRESWICK, F.A.	'Thermal design of Stirling-cycle machines'. The Society of Automotive Engineers international automotive Engineering congress, Detroit, Mich. January 1965.
15	WITTEVEEN, R.A.J.O.	'The Stirling engine, present and future'. UKAEA-ENEA symposium on industrial application for isotopic power generators, Harwell, September 1966.
16		'Air pollution control in transport engines'. IMechE, Solihull, November, 1971.
17	THRING, R.H.	'Fluidised bed combustion'. Private communication, Reading University 1972.
18	DUNN, P.D.	'Alternatives to the IC engine as a means of overcoming atmospheric pollution by road vehicles'. Paper 11a, Engineering-design conference, Southampton 1971.

9   The vapour engine

S.S. Wilson, M.A.
Department of Engineering Science, University of Oxford, England

A vapour-cycle engine possesses the following inherent advantages and disadvantages; whether it can be developed into an effective automotive power plant depends on the extent to which its advantage can be exploited and its disadvantages minimised to effect a successful engineering compromise.

(a)   Being an external-combustion engine, it employs continuous combustion with all the advantages of low atmospheric and noise pollution. The level of exhaust emission already obtained is shown by results published for the Steam Engine Systems (SES) reciprocating steam automotive power plant as part of the USA Environmental Protection Agency (EPA) programme (Table 1).

Table 1

Emissions:	NO_x	0·14 g/mile	(1976 standard = 0·40)
	CO	0·17 g/mile	(1976 standard = 3·40)
	HC	0·03 g/mile	(1976 standard = 0·41)

(b)   The Rankine cycle, as plotted on a temperature/entropy diagram, e.g. Fig. 1, gives a variable heat-reception process over a range of temperature, from about 100°C to 550°C; this leads to a compact and efficient primary heat exchanger, i.e. boiler, giving moderately low maximum temperatures for the tube material and a low exhaust temperature e.g. 125 − 330°C, depending on the load, without the need for a regenerator. These conditions compare very favourably with both gas-turbine and Stirling-engine material requirements.

(c)   The work ratio is high, specially with steam; i.e. the ratio of nett work done in the cycle to positive, expander work; since the feed pump is pumping only liquid, of small volume compared with the vapour, little of the expander work is lost in compression; so the achieved efficiency is close to the ideal cycle efficiency. Vapour cycles thus compare favourably with other engines, particularly gas turbines, where a large proportion of turbine work is lost to the compressor. This explains their poor performance away from design conditions, and also the fundamental difficulty of obtaining a good performance at small powers, where the component efficiency inevitably suffers. By contrast, the vapour cycle is likely to maintain a good efficiency over a range of loads and sizes.

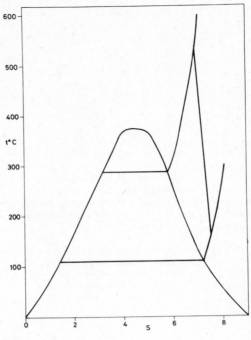

Fig. 1

(d) Several different fluids may be considered for use in a vapour cycle; water is the most obvious, and eminently suitable apart from the need to provide oil lubrication of the cylinder and piston, which have to operate with highly super-heated steam, the consequent need to separate the oil from the feed water, and the problem of freezing during cold weather. The Esso Co. has evolved a usable high-temperature oil, and tests have shown that a small amount of oil in the feed to the boiler does not cause trouble. Two schemes have been worked out for overcoming the freezing problem; both involve draining to a sump, which is either insulated and kept warm by an automatic heater or else made sufficiently flexible to allow freezing without damage.

Two other fluids are being used, and others are being evolved and tested by firms such as Monsanto and du Pont. The reason for seeking such fluids is partly to overcome the freezing problem, partly to achieve better lubrication, and partly to give better expander performance, as discussed below. The fluids in use are designated AEF-78, which has a specific gravity of 1.793 and is used by Aerojet Liquid Rocket Systems (ALRS) in its turbine unit, and Fluorinol ·85 (a mixture of 85% trifluoromethanol with 15% water), used by the Thermo Electron Corporation (TECO - linked with the Ford Motor Co.) in its reciprocating unit. Monsanto has tested a number of fluids and found a 57·5% by weight of pentafluorobenzene and 42·5% of hexafluorobenzene to be satisfactory in most respects, including thermal stability in a 1000 h test at 720°F in a dynamic test loop at 1000 psig (382°C and 70 bar). Du Pont has also developed and tested several potentially useful fluids.

Table 2 shows relevant properties of some fluids currently in use or under test.

122

Table 2

	Water	85% hexafluorobenzene 15% pentafluorobenzene	Monochlorbenzene (CP27)	
Molecular weight	18	175	112.5	
Slush point, deg. C	0	-42	-45	
Boiling point, deg. C	100	78	132	
Latent heat, kJ/kg	2255	184	230	
Condensing pressure at 105°C (bar)	1·2	2·07	0·45	
Liquid density at 100°C, g/ml	1000	1398	1030	kg/m³
Vapour pressure 250°C (bar)	39·7	38·1	10·9	
Specific heat of liquid 100°C, relative to water	1·0	0·330	0·30	
Critical temperature, deg. C	374	236	359	
Critical pressure (bar)	218	37·7	44·3	
Maximum cycle temperature, deg. C	538	378	333	

(e) There is a wide choice of hardware available to carry out the cycle; the choice of boiler seems to have settled on monotube boilers using a finned tube to increase the gas-side heat transfer.

A remarkably compact and efficient boiler has been evolved for the SES steam reciprocating unit: a cylindrical package 18 in. in diameter and 11 in. long, with a heat release of $1·58 \times 10^6$ Btu/h and an efficiency at full load of 85%, based on lower calorific value. It weighs under 100 lb. For the expander, a reciprocating or a rotary positive-displacement machine or a turbine may be used; of the four designs at present supported by the EPA, two use reciprocating machines and two turbines, but Wankel himself is reputed to be working on a rotary steam expander, and the Australian Sarich engine is also a possibility.

The choice of expander is very much linked with the choice of working fluid; for steam in small powers, a reciprocating engine shows appreciably better isentropic efficiency, e.g. 75%, compared with 50-60% for a turbine. With a heavy-molecular-weight fluid, the turbine efficiency can be equal to that of a reciprocator; this is because the reduced nozzle velocity, inversely proportional to square root of the molecular weight, allows the blade speed to be optimum, and the increased mass flow (since $\Delta h \propto \frac{1}{MW}$) allows a full rather than a partial, admission design. One penalty is, of course, the increased feed-pump power needed for a bigger mass flow.

Another difference concerns the rotational speed; the reciprocator tends to be limited to speeds of 2500 rev/min or so, which is low compared with an internal-combustion engine; so a larger and heavier engine than an internal-combustion engine of comparable power output is required; this disadvantage can be offset by using a high steam pressure and so developing a high bmep. The turbine has a very high speed, e.g. 30 000 rev/min, so needs a high-speed reduction gearbox. A rotary expander would run at an intermediate speed, leading to a compact engine-plus-transmission unit. A further possibility is a compound expander formed by means of a reciprocating high-pressure stage exhausting to a rotary second stage, so avoiding the losses due to blowdown after incomplete expansion; this would be a more compact arrangement than a more conventional reciprocator, owing to the high speed of the rotary machine.

123

There is little choice for the condenser, which must be aircooled for a vehicle, and, if it is to condense under all conditions of power and ambient temperature up to 15°C, a high condensing temperature is inevitable, e.g. 105°C. Although the Garrett Corporation has evolved practical solutions* for three of the EPA low-pollution automotive systems, for three different fluids, the necessity to condense at such a high temperature is the chief factor in limiting the thermal efficiency of a vapour-cycle unit; even the old steam locomotive was slightly better off by exhausting steam directly to atmosphere, but it still sacrificed a great deal by not being able to condense to a low temperature, near to ambient, such as is done in a power station (via cooling towers or to a river or the sea) or in a steamship. It is because of this ability to reject heat at a low temperature that a steam turbine can achieve as high an efficiency as the best diesel, gas turbine or Stirling engine but with a top temperature far lower, perhaps even lower than the exhaust temperature for the other engines. This, of course, leads to the idea of a combined cycle that could achieve thermal efficiencies of up to 50% or so, but that is another story; but let it be clearly understood that the only reason a vapour-cycle automotive unit is of limited thermal efficiency is the condenser-cooling problem.

The choice of feed pump is as wide as for the expander, namely reciprocating, rotary or turbomachine. All are in use; the SES system uses a 3-cylinder piston pump, the natural choice for a high-pressure and low-volume flow; another type is a sliding-vane motor with 2-lobe deformable stator, which can be adjusted to maintain pump efficiency over a range of flows.

Faced with such a wide choice of fluid and hardware, can an acceptable automotive power plant be designed? R.M. Palmer of Ricardo and Co. has shown in an earlier design study for General Motors (Reference 1) that, despite the many technical and other problems, a steam reciprocating unit could be designed to power a medium-sized American automobile but that it would not be competitive in performance or in cost. Despite this, EPA has funded four different attempts at producing a vehicle engine of about 150 hp, covering all the major choices of fluid and hardware, namely steam reciprocating, steam turbine, organic reciprocating, organic turbine. Table 3 shows the main features of the four systems funded by EPA. Of these, the steam reciprocating seems furthest ahead at the present moment, and may well be the one to be selected at the end of 1973 for further development. However, it seems unlikely that it could compete on grounds either of cost or of full-load fuel economy with a conventional engine, and, in view of the increased emphasis now on energy conservation, the future development of any vapour-cycle unit for a high-performance vehicle unit appears uncertain.

For a city vehicle in which a limited top speed, e.g. 40 mile/h, is acceptable and for which the normal condition of operation is stopping and starting, a different situation prevails. Because the normal internal-combustion engine is at a severe disadvantage in such conditions, its performance as regards both atmospheric pollution and fuel economy is poor. The fundamental requirements for stop-start operation are: first, energy storage to even out the peak and troughs of power demand and so reduce the size of prime mover and enable it to operate at steady, optimum conditions; secondly, the right form of torque/speed curve. The normal internal-combustion engine fails in both respects, having almost no energy storage and requiring a major transmission system to overcome the basic unsuitability of its torque/speed curve. By contrast, the reciprocating steam engine has some degree of thermal-energy storage and a very suitable torque/speed curve; these advantages are reflected in the acceleration and fuel-consumption curves at speeds up to 30 mile/h (Figs. 2 and 3 from Reference 1.)

*For example, the steam condenser for the SES system has a frontal area 49 x 19 in. and a depth of 4 in., weights 93 lb, and has two fans absorbing a total of 14 hp in low gear, reducing to about 5 hp in top gear

Reference 1. PALMER, R.M. (1969-70): 'An exercise in steam for design', Proc. I. Mech.E., 184 (2A)

Table 3

Main contractor	Steam Engine Systems	Thermo Electric Corp.	Aerojet Liquid Rocket Corp.	Lear Motors Corp.
Fluid	Steam	Fluorinol 85	AEF 78	Steam
Expander	Reciprocator	Reciprocator	Axial turbine	Axial turbine
Dimensions	4 cylinders 3·5 in. bore 3·5 in. stroke	4 cylinders 4·42 in bore x 3·00 in. stroke	5·8 in. diam.	5·4 in. diam.
Maximum pressure psia	1000	700	1000	950
Maximum temperature, deg. F	1000	550	650	1050
Gross horse power	158	146	150	131
Speed, rev/min	2500	1800	32 000	65 000
Parositic power, hp	17	35	44	26
Total weight, lb	923	1236	1210	

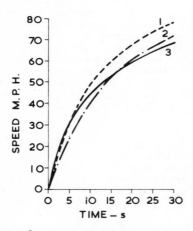

1　With 230 in³ petrol engine and 3-speed manual transmission.

2　With 115 in³ steam engine, 875 lb/h boiler and single-speed transmission (40 mile/h per 1000 rev/min).

3　With 82·5 in³ steam engine, 750 lb/h boiler and 2-speed transmission (20 and 40 mile/h per 1000 rev/min).

Vehicle weight, 3992 lb.

Steam inlet conditions, 1500 lb/in² abs. 900° F.

Condenser pressure 20 lb/in² abs.

Fig. 2　Acceleration curves for Chevelle car, with various power units

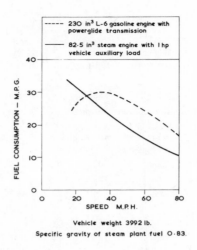

Vehicle weight 3992 lb.

Specific gravity of steam plant fuel 0·83.

Fig. 3 Comparative fuel consumptions of petrol- and steam-engined Chevelle cars at steady speeds

An alternative approach is the hybrid drive, the subject of a later paper. This employs energy storage by means of batteries — much smaller than required for an all-electric vehicle — and a small prime mover whose size is determined largely by the maximum speed and acceleration requirements. This prime mover could be of almost any form — internal-combustion engine, Stirling engine or a vapour-cycle unit. The first two have been tried by General Motors with results that appear adequate for a city vehicle, but development has not proceeded. The vapour turbine hybrid drive has not yet been tried, though it appears attractive, in that a small turbogenerator unit using a heavy-molecular-weight fluid could be made as a fully sealed unit containing no fluid other than the working fluid and giving the possibility of a long life with little or no maintenance.

Such a system could be applied to any city vehicle, or indeed to any stop-start application such as factory and fork-lift trucks and mining duties. Small city cars for private use are probably less attractive than various forms of public-transport vehicle; the most likely use for a hybrid drive is therefore for taxis, delivery vans and buses, all vehicles whose normal use is confined to builtup areas and which could benefit the environment greatly if they could combine low atmospheric with low noise pollution. This the vapour cycle can offer.

Even if a vapour-cycle automotive power unit does not emerge from all this work now under way in the USA — closely watched by European and Japanese, though not, apparently, by British, automobile manufacturers — there should be some useful 'spinoff' for other applications: Chief of these is the marine: use as an alternative to the diesel; both the large steam reciprocator and the steam turbine have largely yielded to the all-conquering diesel engine, but, in small sizes, a modern vapour-cycle unit, making full use of the low temperature of condensation, could now be designed to compete with the diesel on grounds of noise, vibration, safety and convenience. Another challenge is that of a suitable power unit for village use in less developed countries; again, the vapour-cycle unit, either reciprocating steam or a sealed vapour turbine unit offers a possible solution.

126

Part 4

Electric vehicle engines

10 Electric cars — energy storage and conversion

Prof. P.D. Dunn, Ph.D., C.Eng., F.I.Mech.E., F.I.E.E.
Professor of Engineering Science, University of Reading, England

1 Introduction

Recently the growing awareness and concern over the problems of exhaust pollution and automotive noise has caused a renewed interest in possible alternative systems. Also, looking even further ahead, it will become difficult to satisfy the increasing demand for oil for transport applications. In this paper will be considered the current position and future possible development of electrochemical convertors.

The basic prime mover consists of, first, a source of energy — the fuel — and, secondly, a means of converting this energy in a controllable way into mechanical power. Let us first look at energy sources.

2 Primary sources of energy

Since electricity is not itself a primary source of energy, we should first examine the primary sources of energy from which it is derived, since it may turn out that we have merely moved the source of pollution from the car to the power station without achieving any overall benefit.

To assess the size of the energy demand, it is instructive to look at current practice in the USA. Almost exactly one-quarter of the total energy used in the USA is in the form of petrol for road vehicles, principally private cars. Thus we see that, unless there is a marked change in transport pattern, which seems unlikely, transport is likely to remain a major energy consumer.

An idea of the size of the private-car investment is obtained by noting, that the current installed horsepower in US cars amounts to almost 20×10^9 hp, compared with 4×10^8 hp (or 2% of the car hp) in central power stations. It is not too fanciful to imagine that, if all American drivers revved their engines, the dynamos would be generating an amount of electricity comparable to that generated by the national grid.

The figures given in the previous two paragraphs illustrate the magnitude of the problem in finding alternative power sources for cars.

Of the primary fuels, oil and its derivatives offer a safe, easily handled, cheap form of energy having a high energy content per unit mass and volume. There is a great deal to be said for retaining its use in transport applications; the immediate requirement is to develop convertors having improved pollution and noise characteristics. A particular advantage of oil-type fuels is portability, which is an important requirement in transport applications.

128

Of the other primary fuels, coal, natural gas and nuclear power, these do not favour the construction of portable power supplies, and one is left with the alternatives of

(a) generating electricity in central power stations

(b) in the longer term, production of liquid hydrocarbon fuels by one of several chemical processes.

Both fossil fuel and nuclear (fission) power stations are sources of pollution: in the former, sulphur and dust, and, in the latter, the long-term problem of storage of radioactive wastes.

Nevertheless, since central stations are manned by highly trained staff, and are relatively few, adequate antipollution measures should be possible. The development of nuclear fusion would remove the problem of radioactive fission products; there is, however, still some uncertainty on the health hazard resulting from tritium release.

In the very long term, electricity generated by solar-powered satellites might offer completely pollution-free electrical power (Reference 1).

Since the demand for electricity varies during the 24 h period and also with time of year, there is a considerable quantity of offpeak electricity available from an electrical-power system.

For example, the CEGB Annual Report for 1971-72 quotes an annual total generation of around 50% of the total installed capacity. Assuming that a further 25% is available if it is required, this amounts to $3 \cdot 42 \times 10^{11}$ kWh, compared with $1 \cdot 36 \times 10^8$ t annual import of oil. Nuclear power stations with their high capital costs and relatively low fuel and running costs are particularly suited for continuous operation.

We conclude that, for the present discussion, we should restrict our consideration to chemical, particularly liquid hydrocarbon fuels, and to electricity regarded as a fuel.

3 Energy storage

For vehicles that carry their own source of fuel, we are interested in the size and weight of the fuel required for a given journey. This will depend on a number of factors, including how much energy is released by unit mass of fuel, and how efficiently can this energy be converted to mechanical power. Also, is it necessary to carry the oxidant in addition to the fuel — as is the case for the lead-acid battery — or can one use oxygen from the air as is done in the petrol engine? An indication of the relative suitability of various fuels on an energy to weight basis is given in Table 1.

From this Table, we see just how good petrol is, compared with its alternatives. Although nuclear fuels have a very high energy/weight ratio, other considerations, such as cost, minimum size and safety, rule them out for small-vehicle propulsion. Flywheels, and thermal storage, all have merit for special applications, but, in practice, we come down to the chemical fuels as the only really feasible form of energy storage.

129

Table 1

Energy storage

Method	Specific energy Wh/lb	Remarks
Nuclear Energy:		
Fusion		Requires considerable development; unlikely to be developed for small units
Fission	10^9	Unsuitable on grounds of cost, size, safety, control and weight
Radioactive isotopes, e.g. Sr^{90}		Unsuitable on grounds of cost, availability, shielding and safety; also radioactivity cannot be switched off; specific power low
Chemical Energy:*		
Hydrogen†	14 950	Expensive, bulky
Petrol†	5 850	Cheap, available, easy to handle
Methanol†	2 710	
Hydrogen-oxygen (liquid)	1 660	Expensive, heavy
Lithium-chloride (700°C)	1 140	Secondary batteries under development; corrosive, toxic
Sodium-sulphur (300°C)	385	Secondary batteries under development
Lithium-copper-fluoride	746	Secondary batteries under development
Zinc†	560	Cheap; good specific power and energy
Zinc-silver-oxide	208	Expensive
Lead-lead-oxide	85	Low specific energy
Thermal storage:		
Phase change Lithium fluoride	90	Heat transfer problems due to freezing on the extract pipes
Lithium-hydride (848°C)	160	

130

Table 1 (continued)

Method	Specific energy Wh/lb	Remarks
Heat capacity		
Alumina (1500 - 700°C)	75	
Mechanical energy:		
Strain energy		
Steel	1	Specific energy too low
Rubber	10	Bulky
Compressed gas	10	Bulky
Kinetic energy:		
Rotation	14	Gyroscopic effects; loss of energy on standby; high specific power
Magnetic energy:	0.01	Specific energy too low; Bulky; dissipation during standby
Electrostatic energy:	0.006	Specific energy too low

—

*   Specific energy for chemical reactions is the change in Gibbs free energy ($-\Delta G$/lb) for the reaction

†   This figure does not include the weight of atmospheric oxygen

Table 2

Chemical energy at 25°C

Fuel	Oxidant	Theoretical cell voltage V	Theoretical energy Wh/lb
Hydrogen, g	Air	1·23	14 950
Hydrogen, g	Oxygen (1)	1·23	1 660
Petrol, l	Air		5 850
Methanol (CH_3OH), g	Air	1·19	2 710
Methanol, g	Oxygen	1·19	1 086
C_4H_{10}, g	Air	1·12	6 120
C_4H_{10}, g	Oxygen	1·12	1 325
Ammonia (NH_3), g	Air	1·12	2 410
Ammonia (NH_3), g	Oxygen	1·12	1 000
Hydrazine (N_2H_4), g	Air	1·56	2 370
Hydrazine (N_2H_4), g	Oxygen	1·56	1 185
Zinc (Zn)	Air	1·5	560 (50)
Magnesium (Mg)	Air	3·0	1 800
Aluminium (Al)	Air	2·7	2 400
Cadmium (Cd)	Air	1·0	260
Sodium (Na)	Air	2·3	930
Iron (Fe)	Air	1·25	410
Lithium (Li)	Chlorine (Cl_2)	3·40	1 140
Sodium (Na)	Sulphur (S)	2·08	345 - 605
Lithium (Li)	Copper Fluoride (CuF_2)		746
Zinc (Zn)	Silver Oxide (AgO_2)	1·86	208 (40-50)
Zinc (Zn)	Chlorine (Cl_2)	2·12	377
Lead (Pb)	Lead Dioxide (PbO_2)	2·14	85 (10-14)

Electrochemical conversion

When a fuel is burnt in the normal way, the chemical reaction involved is nonisothermal, and, if, as is usual, no work is done, the chemical-energy release will appear as heat, i.e. as random kinetic energy of the products of combustion. This random energy can only be converted into work in some form of heat engine. The limiting conversion efficiency from heat to work is the Carnot efficiency. The attraction of the electro-chemical convertors is that, in principle, no random energy stage need be involved, and chemical energy, one form of directed energy, is converted direct to work. The maximum energy available in a reaction is $-\Delta G$, the change in the Gibbs free energy for the reaction.

The ideal voltage for the reversible reaction V_0 is given by $V_0 = \dfrac{-\Delta G}{nF}$

$-\Delta G$ is the charge in Gibbs free energy/g mole
where n = number of electrons transferred/g mole
F = Faraday (96 500 C/per g mole)

In practice, irreversibilities will reduce the available cell voltage. Important sources of irreversibility include:

(a)   activation polarisation: loss due to high activation energy for electron transfer at the electrode

(b)   concentration polarisation: change in concentration near the electrode surface

(c)   ohmic polarisation: resistive loss in the electrolyte.

These three polarisation losses reduce the onload voltage from the ideal value V_0. In addition, there may be losses in current due to side reactions (current inefficiency), and, in the fuel cell, some loss of fuel due to scavenging flow removing reaction products.

5 Electrochemical Convertors (References 2 - 5)

We can classify electrochemical convertors as follows:

(a)   primary cells *

(b)   secondary cells

(c)   semi fuel cells

(d)   fuel cells

Such cells may be made from any pair of materials that employ an ionic reaction. The maximum energy available from such a reaction is given by the change in Gibbs free energy $-\Delta G$. In practice, irreversible effects reduce the output to less than this figure. The $-\Delta G$ per unit mass is listed in Table 2. Also listed are some values achieved by modern cells. It is seen that modern practice falls considerably below the theoretical upper limit. This discrepancy is due to several factors, such as the mass of the structural materials, leads and electrolyte.

The figures suggest that significant improvement is possible. On the other hand, one should remember that, in spite of intensive efforts over many years, the improvement in specific energy has been small.

* 'Cell' refers to a single electrode; pair or combination of such cells to give higher voltage output are called 'batteries'.

What technical requirements do we require from the cell?

We have already mentioned two important parameters:

(i)   specific energy, which determines the range of the vehicle

(ii)   specific power, which determines performance

The latter is limited by polarisation effects.

Other factors include size, cost, safety, cycle life, and, in the case of storage cells, the recharging time.

We will now briefly survey the present position of electrochemical convertors and mention some of the more promising developments:

5.1 Primary Cells

These are unlikely to be used, owing to the high cost involved, unless means can be developed for anode replacement, e.g. in the zinc-air cell.

5.2 Secondary or Storage Cells

These devices use electricity as fuel.

The most important storage cells are the following:

Lead-acid cell

In spite of the low specific energy mentioned earlier, the lead-acid cell has enjoyed considerable popularity for a number of years, and has been developed to a very advanced stage. It is widely used in delivery vans, fork-lift trucks and other special vehicles. As a result of the high stage of development, the lead-acid cell has the cheapest energy-storage cost of any existing storage system. However, the maximum specific energy is poor, around 10-14 Wh/lb. The specific power of 35 W/lb is again too low to be of interest for large commercial electric cars. The efficiency of storage is about 75%, i.e. 75% of the energy stored in the battery is released to do useful work. The charging efficiency is about 80%. This gives an overall efficiency of energy used to energy input of about 60%.

Nickel-iron cell

The nickel-iron cell, or alkaline cell, so called because it makes use of an alkaline (KOH) electrolyte, has a similar specific energy to that of the lead-acid cell. It is more robust than the latter, will accept repeated deep-discharge cycling, and has specific power of 35 W/lb. Nickel-iron cells are slightly more expensive than lead-acid traction cells.

Nickel-cadmium cell

The nickel cadmium cell is similar to the nickel-iron, but allows much higher discharge rates of typically 75 - 100 W/lb, and up to 300 W/lb for special construction. Energy density of 15-20 Wh/lb is somewhat higher than that of the previous two cells. Cost, however, is high — some five times the cost of the lead-acid traction battery. Nickel-cadmium cells may be charged at a very high rate, and can be fully charged in as short a time as 15 min. The charging efficiency is low.

Silver-zinc cell

The silver-zinc cell offers a very high specific energy, currently 40 - 55 Wh/lb, and a high specific power, 100 W/lb. The cycle life is very short, of the order of 100 cycles or less, and the cost is too high, except for special applications.

Silver-cadmium cell

Silver-cadmium cells have a specific energy currently around 25 Wh/lb. They are, however, even more expensive than silver-zinc, and hence unsuitable for the present application.

New systems under development

When using highly reactive materials such as lithium, spontaneous reactions will occur with aqueous electrolytes, and it is therefore necessary to use either organic electrolytes or molten solids.

Lithium-chlorine cell (Reference 8)

The lithium-chlorine cell, currently in development by General Motors in the USA offers a specific power of 150 W/lb and a specific energy of 100 - 200 Wh/lb. Unfortunately, it requires to be operated at a temperature of around $650°C$ and poses serious compatibility problems, and will probably be of high cost.

Zinc-chloride cell (Reference 7)

The zinc-chlorine couple listed in Table 2 offers a high specific energy of theoretical value 377 Wh/lb. The material costs are low, the cell voltage high 2·12 V, and the reaction is electrochemically active at around ambient temperature and pressure. The reaction is also readily reversible. Until recently, the reaction has not been seriously considered owing to the difficulty in storing chlorine. A new development is the use of chlorine hydrate, a solid formed by bubbling chlorine through water. C.J. Amati, of the Oxymetal Finishing Company, has reported on the construction of a 24-cell sub-module battery of 1 kWh energy.

A larger assembly producing 100 A at 200 V was later installed in a Vega Hatchback.

The projected performance for production systems is as follows:

Specific energy (4 h rate)	50 – 75 Wh/lb
Specific power	40 – 60 W/lb
Energy density (4 h rate)	3 Wh/in^3
Cost	0·01 $/Wh
Life	100 000 miles

Sodium-sulphur cell (Reference 9)

The sodium-sulphur cell again offers the possibility of a very high performance, typically 100 W/lb. and 150 Wh/lb. It requires to be operated at around 300°C, and again poses some compatibility problems. The reactants, sulphur and sodium, are cheap, and the cost may be reduced to an acceptable level. Early work was carried out on this battery by the Ford Motor Company of the USA. More recently, the CEGB has further developed this cell at its Capenhurst laboratories.

5.3 Semi fuel cell (Reference 7)

From Table 2, it is seen that metal-air cells, using lithium, magnesium, aluminium, sodium or zinc, all offer high specific energies. Considerable effort has gone into developing the zinc-air cell and a specific energy around 50 Wh/lb has been achieved. 70 - 80 Wh/lb may be possible with further development. Problems include:

(i)   limited cycle life

(ii)   difficulty in ensuring reversibility of the oxygen electrode

(iii)   contamination by CO_2 from the air

Leesona Moos has developed a primary zinc-air cell with replaceable anode. A figure of 100 Wh/lb has been quoted for energy density. However, the practical problems of handling electrodes soaked in caustic soda are a severe limitation to its use.

5.4 Fuel cell (References 10-14)

Like the primary and secondary cell, the fuel cell converts fuel and oxidant to electrical energy by electrochemical reaction. The fuel cell differs from the former, in that fuel and oxidant are stored externally and the electrodes serve merely as sites for the ionic reactions. The fuel cell offers the advantage of a considerable weight reduction over the secondary cell, though the volume is similar. Fuel cells have a number of advantages as energy convertors. They are not subject to the Carnot limitation on efficiency. They offer the prospect of low noise, long life and low maintenance. Currently, however, their cost is high.

The basic fuel cell is shown in Fig. 1. It consists of:

(i)   electrodes

(ii)   electrolyte

(iii)   fuel

(iv)   oxidant

(v)   ancillaries — circulating pumps, heat exchangers, instrumentation and control, etc.

Let us look at these items separately.

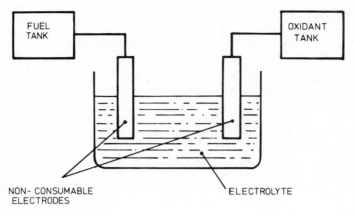

FUEL TANK

OXIDANT TANK

NON- CONSUMABLE ELECTRODES

ELECTROLYTE

Fig. 1   Fuel cell

Electrodes

The reaction mechanism in a fuel cell is a 3-phase reaction between solid electrode, liquid electrolyte and gaseous fuel. The reaction area should be as large as possible, and hence porous electrodes are used. It is necessary to prevent flooding by the electrolyte into the gas feed. This is usually achieved in one of two ways. Bacon adopted the two pore size electrode in which the pore size is changed from $20\mu m$ on the gas side to $2\mu m$ on the electrolyte side. The second method is wet-proofing part of the electrode by means of a hydrophobic coating. The electrode should be a good conductor of electricity, and should also be compatible chemically with the electrolyte. It should either provide a catalytic reaction itself or serve as a support for a catalyst.

Nickel, stainless steel, carbon and metalised porous plastics (Porvic) have all been used with aqueous alkaline electrolytes. With acid electrolytes, carbon and porous plastics have been used.

Electrolyte

Early fuel cells made use of aqueous alkaline electrolytes, particularly KOH. If unscrubbed air is used as an oxidant, or where hydrocarbon fuels are used, it is necessary to select an acid electrolyte, since carbonates are formed in an alkaline electrolyte. It is found that acid electrolytes require heavier catalyst loadings and also present incompatibility problems. Molten salts have been used as electrolytes, but require temperatures in the range $1000 - 1250^{\circ}C$. For low-power-density cells, ion-exchange resin membranes have been developed, but would not be suitable for the present application.

Fuel

Most successful fuel cells have made use of gaseous hydrogen, which has high reaction energy and reactivity. It is, however, inconvenient to store, being both heavy and bulky. Some workers have operated hydrogen fuel cells using hydrogen produced by reforming ammonia or methanol. Hydrazine dissolved in the electrolyte has also been used, as has methanol. Hydrogen operated at temperatures around $200^{\circ}C$ with activated nickel electrodes does not require an additional catalyst. If used at lower temperatures, $0\cdot5 - 3$ mg/cm^2 platinum of superficial electrode surface is necessary when used with aqueous alkaline electrolytes. Hydrazine dissolved in an aqueous electrolyte does not require a noble-metal catalyst. Current densities around 100 ma/cm^2 have been reported at temperatures as low as 0°C.

With methanol and sulphuric acid electrolyte at $70 - 90^o$C, current densities of 100 mA/cm^2 have been achieved, but heavy $20 - 50$ mg/cm^2 (platinum ruthenium) catalysts were required.

Oxidant

Gaseous oxygen is the most suitable oxidant, though, to reduce weight atmospheric air may be used. CO_2 must be scrubbed from this air if used with an alkaline electrolyte. A further disadvantage with atmospheric air is the additional circulator size.

6   Conclusions

The position on batteries is summarised qualitatively in Table 3, taken from Reference 7, and in Fig. 2 taken from Reference 6.

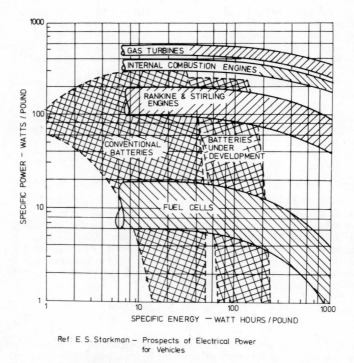

Ref: E. S. Starkman — Prospects of Electrical Power
for Vehicles

Fig. 2   Comparative performance of various power systems

Table 3 (Reference 7)

Outlook for various batteries

System	Energy density	Power density	Rechargeability or refuelability	Service life	Material availability	Cost	Other problems
Lead-acid	Poor	Good	Good	Good	Excellent	Excellent	–
Nickel-iron	Poor	Fair	Good	Excellent	Good	Fair	–
Nickel-cadmium	Poor	Excellent	Excellent	Excellent	Poor	Poor	–
Silver-zinc	Fair	Excellent	Poor	Poor	Poor	Poor	–
Zinc-air	Good	Fair	Good	Fair(?)	Excellent	Good	Complexity of maintenance (?)
Magnesium-air	Excellent	Fair	Fair(?)	?	Excellent	Excellent	Refuelling is mechanical
Lithium-organic electrolyte	Excellent	Poor	Fair to good	Fair (?)	Good	Good	–
Sodium-sulphur	Good to excellent	Excellent	Excellent	Excellent	Excellent	Excellent	Safety, high temperature, startup
Lithium-chlorine	Excellent	Excellent	Excellent	Excellent	Good	Good	Safety, toxicity, complexity, startup(?)
Lithium-tellurium	Excellent	Excellent	Excellent	Excellent	Poor(?)	Poor	Temperature toxicity, startup(?)

139

To date, successful fuel cells have employed reactive fuels such as hydrogen or hydrazine, often in association with high temperatures and expensive catalysts. Although there are still difficult constructional materials problems to be solved, the major development required is in the field of cheap catalysts to allow the use of cheaper liquid fuels, in particular methanol.

7   References

Solar power

1   GLASER, P.E.: 'Satelite solar power station', Solar Energy, 1969, **12**, pp.353-61

General

2   BARAK, M.: 'Developments in electrochemical energy-conversion devices, batteries and fuel cells', Proc. IEE 1965, **112**, ( ), pp.

3   GILMAN, A.: 'Stored electricity' (Macmillan, 1971) chap. 13

4   BARAK, M.: 'Fuel cells' (Macmillan, 1971), chap. 14

5   LIEBHAFSKY, H.A., and CAIRNS, E.J.: 'Fuel cells and fuel batteries', (Wiley, 1968)

6   STARKMAN, E.S.: 'Prospects of electric power for vehicles', SAE San Franscisco, August 1968

Zinc-chloride cells

7   AMATO, C.J.: Paper 730248, SAE congress, Detroit, January 1973

Metal-air cells

8   GREGORY, D.P.: 'Metal air batteries', Paul Mills & Boon Ltd., 1972

Lithium-chlorine cells

9   RIGHTMIRE, R.A.: 'A sealed lithium chloride fused salt secondary battery', SAE conference, Detroit, January 1969

Sodium-sulphur cells

10   KUMMER, J.T., and WEBER, N.: A sodium sulphur secondary battery', SAE conference, Detroit, 1967

Hydrox fuel cells

11   BACON, F.T.: 'Fuel cells', in YOUNG, G.J. (Ed.): Vol. 1 (Reinhold, 1960), chap. 5

Hydrocarbon and methanol fuel cells

12   WILLIAMS, K.R.: 'Hydrocarbon and methanol low temperature fuel cell system' in COLLINS, D.H. (Ed.) 'Power sources', (Pergamon Press, 1968)

13   GILLEBRAND, M.I., and LOMAX, G.R.: 'The hydrazine fuel cell' in COLLINS, D.H.
     'Batteries' (Ed.): (Pergamon Press, 1963)

14   WILLIAMS, K.R., ANDREW, M.R., GRESSLER, W.J., and JOHNSON, J.K.: Paper
     700022. SAE conference, Detroit, January 1970

15   SAE J., 1968, **76**, (12), p.61

11   Electric cars—present state of development and future prospects

Prof. P.D. Dunn , Ph.D., C.Eng., F.I.Mech.E., F.I.E.E.
Professor of Engineering Science, University of Reading, England

1   Alternatives to the internal-combustion engine

1.1   The problem

Any major change in the transport pattern will have marked sociological and industrial repercussions, and will require major capital investment. The electric car is one of several technically feasible alternative possibilities. Others include the Stirling-cycle and Rankine-cycle external-combustion engines, either used alone or in combination with storage batteries in the form of hybrid power systems. The principal motivation behind any change will be the reduction of pollution and noise. A further factor of increasing importance is the conservation of primary energy sources. Change to external-combustion engines will result in an improvement in noise and pollution, and will require detailed changes in fuel production, and the manufacturing and servicing industries. A shift to electric cars using storage batteries and hence electricity as fuel would involve a more major change in the manufacturing and servicing industries, and oil, if it continued to be used for this purpose, would be burnt in central power stations. If fuel cells are adopted methanol is likely to be the preferred fuel, and its production and distribution would be similar to the present system. The manufacturing and servicing industries would, of course, require major change.

Long term, one must ask the question: 'What will be the transport pattern of the future?' It seems likely that fast 200-300 mile/h links will be set up between main population centres. The Takaido 130 mile/h train is an early example of such a development, and studies on more advanced systems are being conducted in the UK, the USA and elsewhere. With such a transport system, a major problem will be that of transporting both groups and individuals for short distances around the termini. A number of possibilities have been put forward (Reference 1) including moving pavements and small self-drive taxis. Public transport may not be acceptable to all, and it seems likely that, for a long time, there will be a dual requirement, some requiring personal long-distance transport, others accepting public transport over long distances, provided that there are adequate terminal transport facilities.

For the first category, the long-distance public-transport terminal facilities can be provided by small self-drive taxis. Such vehicles could use electrical batteries, and are well within the capabilities of present-day technology.

For travellers who prefer their own vehicles for the whole journey, a possible solution is an electrical vehicle that may be driven from home to the motorway using battery power. Such a vehicle could be constructed with the ability to join the main trunk road, transferring to automatic control and utilising power from fixed lines — returning to manual self-powered operation for the final phase of the journey. There does not seem to be any major technical difficulty preventing the development of such a system.

142

If this is to be the likely future transport pattern, it would seem sensible to take steps to achieve general acceptability for the low-cost, low-performance, short-range vehicle. Such vehicles may be a commercial proposition at the present time as second or commuter cars.

Although the above may well be desirable in the long term and for the general good of the community, in the short term there is the problem of gaining acceptance from the individual motorist. We should therefore look, first, at the characteristics of the internal-combustion (i.c.) engined car.

In the short term, it is necessary to accept the present pattern of transport, and any alternative to the i.c. engine will need to show clear advantages over it under present-day conditions. One should therefore ask what the requirements are and how the i.c. engine meets them. One difficulty, of course, is that present-day requirements have grown round the capabilities of the i.c. engine, and are therefore well matched to it. The average motorist has the basic requirements from a prime mover, that it should perform its work adequately, cheaply and safely. These requirements imply that the following conditions should be satisfied:

(a) Driveability: This includes the convenience factors, such as rapid starting, simple controls, reliability, readily available maintenance. Also included are the performance capabilities that are partly required to give a short journey time and partly to enable the motorist to maintain a position relative to other traffic; the latter is an important safety consideration. We should note that a considerable power load is demanded by the auxiliaries, particularly the heater. This requirement presents a real difficulty when one is using a high-efficiency conversion system.

(b) Economy: Cost is made up of capital amortised over life, fuel and efficiency and maintenance.

(c) Safety: The i.c. engine has the advantage of using a nontoxic fuel, which can be handled safely. The engine itself is also reasonably safe; i.e. it is not likely to explode, nor leak toxic or dangerous materials.

2   The electric car

A number of the designs referred to later are conversions of petrol-engined cars to electric propulsion. In making such a conversion, one tends to compound the limitations of both types of power supply. For example, if, in a design, we accept a low top speed, we no longer require the same road-holding and suspension characteristics; this both cheapens the design and provides more geometrical flexibility. One feature that might profitably be introduced in a small 'second car' is the concept of plug-in units, e.g. golf carts, shopping trolleys in which a child could be permanently seated etc.

A characteristic that should be exploited is the potentially long life of the propulsion unit (less the battery) and its relative freedom from maintenance. Coupled with a lightweight plastic/light-alloy structure a life of 20 years should be possible.

Since the major problems are those of energy storage and conversion, we will now examine these in more detail.

3 Energy storage

We considered the existing energy-storage systems and also those under development in the previous paper (Reference 2); we saw that the following are commercially available:

(i)   Lead-acid battery: well developed, reliable, inexpensive; specific energy 10 - 14Wh/lb; specific power 10 - 35W/lb; good recycling life

(ii) Nickel-iron battery: well developed, reliable, robust; similar in specific energy to lead-acid battery but more expensive, poor low-temperature performance, no advantages over the lead-acid battery for this application

(iii) Nickel-cadmium battery: somewhat higher specific energy than the lead-acid battery but several times more expensive; also requires cadmium, which is relatively scarce material; offers very high specific power (75-100 W/lb, possibly up to 300 W/lb); in addition to this high discharge current, these batteries can be recharged at a high current and hence have a rapid recharge time; good recycling life; can be useful, used in association with lead-acid batteries to improve overall specific power

(iv) Silver-zinc battery: very high specific energy (40 -55 Wh/lb) and specific power (100 W/lb), but suffers from short recycling life, order of 100 cycles, and is prohibitively expensive for present application.

Thus, for the immediate future, we are restricted to the lead-acid battery, possibly backed by nickel-cadmium batteries for providing power peaks.

In the future, batteries of higher specific energy will be developed by making use of either/or air electrodes (the semifuel cells) and lightweight metals such as sodium or lithium. These developments hold out the promise of realising specific energy greater than 100 Wh/lb and specific power greater than 100 W/lb, which are necessary to give an overall performance comparable to that of the i.c. engine.

(v)   Zinc-air battery: currently 50 Wh/lb with possibility of improvement to 70 or 80 Wh/lb; the recycling life is not yet satisfactory; other metal-air combinations offer the possibility of greater specific energy, but are at an earlier stage of development

(vi) Sodium sulphur: offers both high specific energy (150 Wh/lb) and specific power (100 W/lb); requires to be operated at a temperature of 300°C and will have startup problems. Corrosion will require careful selection of constructional materials. The basic reactants are cheap, and there is the possibility of a good recycling life. There may be a safety hazard in the event of a collision

(vii) Lithium-chlorine battery: offers the possibility of both high specific energy (100 - 200 Wh/lb) and high specific power (150 W/lb); requires an even higher temperature than the sodium-sulphur battery (650°C).

(viii)Zinc-chlorine battery: offers the possibility of 50 - 75 Wh/lb and 40 - 60 W/lb at ambient temperature and cheap materials. There may be a safety hazard.

All the above energy-storage devices are subject to the two basic limitations of storage batteries: they require to be charged electrically, and the battery size determines both the energy stored and the power output.

144

The remaining possibility is the fuel cell, which does not suffer from either of the above limitations, but does require heat exchangers, pumps and other ancillaries.

(ix)   Hydrox fuel cell: the most developed, reliable and best understood of the fuel cells. Even this cell has a rather poor specific power 10 - 20 Wh/lb, and requires an expensive and bulky fuel, hydrogen. The cell must either be operated hot (200°C) or make use of expensive catalysts.

(x)   Hydrogen fuel cells: the hydrocarbon may be reformed to give hydrogen, which is burnt in a Hydrox fuel cell, or burnt directly in a high-temperature cell. The former is both bulky and expensive, and the latter is in an early development stage. Neither offers the hope of a cheap system. A further possibility is the use of methanol dissolved in the electrolyte. This requires the discovery of a cheap catalyst before it can be considered as a realistic possibility.

4   Electric motors and control

To convert the electrical energy into mechanical shaft power, we require an electric motor, together with a transmission system and means of control. Overall efficiency of this conversion system is clearly very important, and weight may have to be increased to permit greater efficiency, since it is likely that the motors and control will be lighter than the battery system.

(a)   Motors (References 3 and 4)

Both conventional d.c. or a.c. motors may be used. The specific power of the motor will be determined by its speed, which in turn is limited by the form of construction. A.C. motors may be operated at higher speeds than d.c. motors. It is unlikely that printed-circuit motors will be adopted, because of the speed restriction due to the large-diameter rotor. The homopolar motor is of interest, but is a high-current low-voltage device, and the control of these high currents may be both expensive and bulky.

(b)   Control (Reference 5)

Solid-state devices are suitable for use with either d.c. or a.c. motors. The invertor required for the a.c. motor tends to be larger and more expensive than the chopper required for the d.c. motor. On the other hand, brushware problems are eliminated in the latter. In both cases, regeneration is possible, and can lead to useful energy saving with resulting range increase. It has been suggested (Reference 6) that there may be some advantage in using a continuously variable mechanical speed control together with a shunt-wound d.c. motor operating at its optimum frequency as an alternative to the solid-state-controlled variable-speed motor. This technique was used in the Shell DAF conversion (Reference 14).

(c)   Charging problem

The requirement to charge electric storage batteries is a major difficulty in the introduction of battery-powered cars. For a small car of typically 6 kWh capacity, assuming an 80% charging efficiency would require about 8 kWh. If charged overnight, a 1 kW charger would be suitable. The cost of this charger must be added to the cost of the power supply. Apart from the inconvenience of the charging time, the location of the charger is obviously of importance. It is sometimes suggested that very rapid charging is possible; apart from the requirement on the battery to accept the rapid charge, the increased cost of the charger and power supply rules it out for the private motorist. Again, rapid in this context is possibly 15 - 30 min, which compares unfavourably with the time currently necessary to refuel the petrol tank. It seems that a certain amount of inconvenience in charging is inevitable.

5   Hybrids

It may be possible to combine the advantages of two separate systems to produce an overall system, a hybrid, having performance superior to either individual system. For example, the high specific energy of the fuel cell, together with the high specific power of the storage battery, is a possible combination. The use of internal or external combustion engines operating at constant power output and maximum efficiency in association with storage batteries has also been considered. An example is the General Motors Stir-lec, a 8 hp engine acting as the battery charger for a bank of lead-acid batteries, which in turn drive a 20 hp induction motor. A further advantage is that the vehicle can run entirely on batteries for town use. Again, if the batteries become discharged, they may be recharged in situ from the engine. The efficiency of the hybrid is high, since the engine always operates at full load; on the other hand, capital cost is likely to be higher than for single systems, particularly for small vehicles.

6   Present state of development

The history of the electric car extends back to before either the steam- or the petrol-engined car. The first practical electric car reported was by Robert Davidson of Aberdeen in 1837, and, in 1898, an electric car held the land speed record of 39·24 mile/h., a record that was raised to 65·79 mile/h a year later. Recently, the Autolite-Ford Parts Division of the Ford Motor Company in the USA has constructed the Lead Wedge (Reference 7), a high-speed vehicle powered by lead-acid batteries and reported to have attained a speed of 138·862 mile/h and a peak power of 90 kW. Commercial electric vehicles are extensively used; for example, in the UK there are some 45 000 vehicles of the milk-float and delivery-van type in use. Such vehicles have a load capacity of around 0·5 to 2·0 tons and a maximum speed of around 20 mile/h. They have the advantage over the conventional i.c. engine of low fuel and maintenance costs, and long life. They are particularly suited to the frequent stop-start requirement of delivery vehicles. Electric propulsion is also widely used for powering fork-lift trucks and other small vehicles, such as golf carts. However, in spite of the long history of electric-car development, the large development efforts of the past decade, and the extensive use of electric propulsion in special applications, the general situation is disappointing. A number of small cars using lead-acid batteries and having limited range and performance have been constructed, but, to date, no efforts have been made to manufacture such vehicles on a large scale. Several higher-perform-ance, larger vehicles have also been reported. These prototypes have employed advanced-design batteries and also fuel cells. Some of these developments are summ-arised below.

The Ford Comuta is typical of the small-car designs. It was developed by Ford in the UK as an urban car. It has a weight of 1200 lb, a range of 40 miles, maximum speed of 30 mile/h, and uses two 5 hp motors with thyristor control. Lead-acid batteries supply the energy. An interesting feature in the Comuta is the use of waste heat to warm the vehicle. More recently, Enfield Automotive in the Isle of Wight has developed the Enfield 8000, a small car intended for urban use. An early electric vehicle in the USA was the Henney Kilowatt, built by National Union Electric Corporation from the early 1960s. The Henney Kilowatt has a range of about 40 miles, a maximum speed of 40 mile/h, and is powered by 800 lb. of lead-acid batteries; the car used a Renault as the basic vehicle. A number of other firms in the USA have developed very similar designs by converting Renaults. Other designs in the USA include the modification of a Simca by Chrysler Corporation, and a small, 3-door town car, the Delta, by General Electric (Reference 9). All the previous vehicles use lead-acid batteries; various control methods are employed, including thyristor and resistance switching. In the Delta, nickel-cadmium cells provide peak power.

146

Turning now to more advanced designs, in the USA (1966), General Motors has converted a Corvair to electric propulsion (Reference 10). This is interesting, in that silver-zinc batteries were used. The battery weight was 680 lb, and operated a single a.c. induction motor capable of 100 hp for only 130 lb weight.

The performance is similar to that of the unconverted Corvair, though the range between charges is reduced to 40 - 80 miles, from 250 - 300 miles for the petrol-driven version. Other major disadvantages are battery cost, limited number of recharge cycles (100), and the weight of the invertor (235 lb). The Capenhurst Laboratories of the CEGB recently reported the operation of a van powered by sodium-sulphur batteries. The battery power is 50 kW and energy 50 kWh. The battery operating temperature is 350°C, and the electrolyte a   alumina. In the USA a Vega has been fitted with a zinc-chloride battery by the Oxy Metal Finishing Corporation (Reference 11). The original curb weight was raised from 2380 to 4614 lb. On a test run, a range of 152 miles was achieved at a steady speed of 50 mile/h, and a peak speed of 66 mile/h achieved over six miles. The peak speed corresponds to a power of 30 kW.

Work on fuel cells has been reported; the earliest reference to a fuel cell operated vehicle is the Allis Chalmers tractor in 1959 (Reference 12). In this vehicle, a natural-gas or propane-fuelled cell supplied 15 kW to drive a 20 hp motor. Another early development by General Motors is the Electrovan in (Reference 13) 1966 a converted GMC Handivan in which Union Carbide Hydrogen oxygen fuel cells are employed, the fuel and oxidant being stored in liquid form in cryogenic containers. Though a very fine technical achievement, it is nevertheless true that the whole of the van, apart from the driver's and front passenger's seats, is occupied by the cell and its ancillary gear. An important feature of the fuel cell is its ability to withstand overload. In this case, the nominally 32 kW cell was capable of supplying a peak power of 160 kW.

Shell in the UK reports (Reference 14) the use of a fuel cell in a converted Daf. A hybrid arrangement was adopted combining two 120-cell hydrazine fuel cells with six 6-call lead-acid batteries to provide peak power. It is also of interest to compare this car with the electric battery-powered cars described earlier. It is found that in terms of acceleration and top speed, the Daf compares favourably with such vehicles, for use as a town vehicle. However, for such a design to become commercially feasible, it will be necessary to find an alternative to the toxic and expensive hydrazine; methanol would provide a very acceptable fuel, but, before it can be used, a suitable and cheap catalyst will need to be developed.

An interesting proposal is that of the Alden Self-Transit Systems Corporation in the USA, who has developed the StaRRcar (self-transit rail and road car), an electrically powered vehicle designed to run on the road under battery power and on a specially designed rail track using an electrical pickup from a distribution system. The vehicle has a top speed of 30 - 40 mile/h when using its lead-acid batteries and a predicted speed of 60 mile/h on the rail track. It seats three passengers and weighs 1700 lb.

7   Conclusions

The basic problem of electric cars is that of energy storage. It seems clear that conventional batteries are unable to supply either the specific power and, more particularly, the specific energy required by conventional cars. Batteries under development, for example the alkali-metal-halogen batteries, hold out promise of reasonable cost and acceptable power and energy capability. They are, however, still some way off, and have the disadvantage of requiring a high operating temperature, using potentially dangerous materials, and posing material-compatibility problems.

Fuel cells, although having a good specific energy, have a low specific power. It should, however, be remembered that they can, for short periods, give a peak power of at least three times their rated power. Current developments involve either expensive catalysts or high temperatures, and do not seem promising for the present application.

Developments in high-speed motors and solid-state control systems are encouraging, though the price and size of the latter will need to be reduced.

Auxiliaries, particularly the heater, are a potentially serious drain on the energy store. A problem with batteries, but not with fuel cells, is the charging equipment, which can be both inconvenient and expensive.

It is difficult to estimate the cost of an electrically powered vehicle relative to the i.c.-engined version. Some estimates suggest that the small car, specially designed rather than converted, may, in fact, be cheaper than the i.c. version. A more realistic estimate may be that the cost of an electrically propelled car, less the battery, will be about the same as for the conventional car, and that the cost of the battery per lb of the alkali metal batteries is unlikely to fall much below the cost of the lead-acid battery.

One concludes that conventional batteries are well suited to power small low-performance short-range vehicles. Later developments may enable high-performance vehicles comparable to the present i.c.-engined car to be produced.

One asks the question: Why do we need alternatives to the conventional i.c. engine? The prime reason is to reduce, or eliminate, the contribution to atmospheric pollution by these engines. Since the private motorist is influenced largely by considerations of performance, cost etc., such an alternative must be at least as good as the i.c. engine in these respects or be assisted by legislation or some form of selective tax, or by prohibition in certain areas, such as town centres.

It seems clear that neither the Stirling engine nor the Rankine engine can compete strongly with the i.c. engine for private cars. Also, the development costs would be very high. Their pollution performance is much better, but they do nevertheless, produce some carbon monoxide and oxides of nitrogen, and possibly hydrocarbons. Also, of course, they produce carbon dioxide. It is not at all clear that, by devoting more effort to the pollution characteristics of i.e. engines, similar performance could be obtained more cheaply and certainly more quickly.

The present-day electric car cannot compete on performance with a car driven by an i.c. engine. However, it may well have a commercial market as a small low-cost low-performance short-range second car. Developments such as the Enfield will fit this role. An important further factor is the long-term role of the electric car. It does not itself produce pollution, neither does its primary energy source, if this is fission or fusion.

If the transport pattern of the future is to be based on nuclear energy, it is important to ensure that short-term developments are consistent with this pattern. For this reason, it would appear to be highly desirable to promote acceptance of the electric vehicle in areas where it can now fill a role, progressively developing and taking advantage of technical advances to increase its use.

There are various measures that might be taken. Tax and legislation have already been mentioned. Government and nationalised industries might consider specifying the use of electric vehicles for their fleets; e.g. the Post Office. Research and development in the problems of electric cars — energy storage, control, conversion and transmission — should be encouraged.

The better the range and performance of the car, the more popular it will become. There are, however, today no technical limitations to the performance of the electric-motor-driven car if it can be connected to external power lines. The StaRRcar, mentioned in Section 6, is an encouraging step in this direction.

One can summarise the conclusions as follows:

(i)   Only electric cars really offer hope as a satisfactory long-term solution in technical, economic and health terms.

(ii) A great deal of development is required before electric cars can achieve technical and economic acceptability.

(iii) The rate of development could be accelerated partly by legislation and partly by increasing research and development funds, particularly into the development of electrochemical cells, both storage batteries and fuel cells.

8   References

1.   RICHARDS, B.: 'New movements in cities' (Studio Vista, London, 1966).

2.   DUNN, P.D.: 'Electric cars — energy storage and conversion'. Paper K, Conference on developments in automotive power plants to reduce fuel consumption, air pollution and noise, London, April 1973

3.   MARCH, J.W.: IEE, symposium on electric vehicles, London, April 1967

4.   WHEELER, C.M.: Paper 690126. SAE, January 1969

5.   HARTMAN: Paper 690127, SAE, January 1969

6.   MANGAN, N.F., GRIFFITH J.T.: Electrical times, 10th December 1971

7.   Ford Autolite news release

8.   MARKLAND, L., LYNES, A.E., and FOOTE, L.R.: Paper 680428, SAE midyear meeting, Detroit, May 1968

9.   LAUMEISTER, B.R.: Paper 680430, SAE midyear meeting, Detroit, May 1968

10. General Motors 'Electrovair II'. General Motors engineering staff, May 1969

11. AMATO, C.J.: Paper 730248, SAE meeting, Detroit, January 1973

12. Union Carbide news release, November 1966

13. Electrovan paper presented at SAE meeting, January 1967

14. ANDREW, M.R., GRESSLER, W.J., JOHNSON J.K., SHORT R.T., and WILLIAMS K.R.: Paper 720191, SAE meeting, Detroit, January 1972

15. Data Sheets. Alden Self-Transit Systems Corporation

Part 5

Discussion and conclusions

M.S. Janota, Ph.D., M.Sc., Dipl. Ing., C.Eng., M.I.Mech.E.

The aim of the conference was to present the current development stages of different types of prime mover suitable for vehicle applications and to discuss future development potential regarding fuel economy and pollutant emission. Recognising the limitations and advantages of each power plant, it is still difficult to predict the future trend in vehicle-engine adaption and development. Environmental requirements, the fuel shorgage, legislation, new inventions and political conflicts are all factors that can suddenly change the well-known trends and reverse or guide them in a completely unexpected direction.

One conclusion that emerged from the conference was the distinction between the consideration of the immediate future, covering the period of the availability of crude-oil and natural-gas resources (say up to year 2000), and the long-term period exploring the utilisation of fossil-fuel resources and nuclear energy (say after year 2000). When looking at the short-term solutions, one cannot exclude the long-term factors, and in particular legislation, which will have a dominant influence on the long-term solutions. Panic measures adopted in the USA to curb the environmental evil clashed with the rising fuel crisis requirements, which led to controversial development trends of automotive power plant. Problems of fuel consumption, fuel availability, as well as air pollution and noise, should be considered in the light of the needs and wishes of the developing countries who will influence the future. Any legislation restricting liquid fuel use to preserve premium fuels for transport, and leading to restrictions in the use of the private car, must coincide with legislation improving public transport. In other words, tax incentives should be directed toward encouragement of the use of railways and other means of public transport.

1 Short-term period

1.1 Nonsteady internal-combustion engines

The compression-ignition engine (diesel) is well-established for power generation on land and as a power plant for traction and marine applications. It has gained dominance in small, stationary power-generating sets and standby units. It also competes very successfully with the gas turbine, even for large power units where fuel economy is more important than the advantage of power/weight ratio. In the traction field, the diesel engine established itself as a highly versatile power plant capable of operating efficiently at a wide range of off-design loads and speeds. In marine applications, it has replaced steam power to a large extent, and the largest units deliver almost all the power required to drive a single ship's propeller. At present it is the most efficient version of the internal-combustion engine, and there is scope for improving the power/weight ratio still further by a higher level of the turbocharging. It is also capable of running successfully on residual fuels and of improving its reliability and noise emission problem by further extensive research and development.

150

For automotive applications, the 4-stroke turbocharged version with a swirl-chamber combustion system shows great promise in meeting the USA 1976 legislation, while giving acceptable performance and a reduced specific fuel consumption. With future stringent pollutant legislation, and the requirement of an economical use of fuels, the diesel engine has an opportunity to spread from the successful heavy commercial vehicle application to the passenger car or light truck (by replacing the spark-ignition gasoline engine).

The compound, or the differential-compound, engine presents a further sophistication of the diesel engine to achieve maximum fuel economy and the most suitable vehicle torque characteristics. However, the increased cost and complexity might make it a less attractive proposition.

The spark-ignition engine, which at present dominates the passenger-car field, has a difficult task ahead to maintain its position, in view of the problems of air pollution and fuel shortage. Complex exhaust cleaning devices can just satisfy the US pollution legislation, with the penalty of increased specific fuel consumption. Research and development work to reduce emission and improve performance by means of fuel injection and stratified charge combustion shows some promise in emission control, but no appreciable improvement in fuel economy. On the other hand, a small relaxation in pollution legislation (NO_x) can lead to significant fuel economy.

An alternative approach using different types of fuel, such as liquid hydrogen or alcohol-gasoline mixtures, could eliminate or reduce pollutant emission and also make a significant contribution to preserving liquid fuel resources. Experimental work has been carried out at Queen Mary College using a 2:1 methanol-isobutanol mixture (a convenient product of the alcohol synthesis from natural gas) as an additive to lead-free gasoline. The results indicate that no change in engine performance is caused with up to 20% alcohol addition, and an exhaust-gas analysis shows that, besides the elimination of lead, other pollutants are also reduced. Increasing the alcohol content above 20% raises the useful compression ratio, and this can be utilised to improve the specific fuel consumption and thermal efficiency of the spark-ignition engine, and it permits successful introduction of turbocharging.

The commercial breakthrough in the development of the rotary engine was achieved by the introduction of the Wankel engine as a suitable power plant for the passenger car. Although a successful solution to the pollutant emission can be effected by the use of external cleaning devices, the problem of its poorer fuel economy still remains a difficult obstacle to overcome.

Rotary engines based on the orthodox reciprocating principle, like the 'Anidyne engine', seem to show more promise, but unfortunately none of this type of engine has yet reached the commercial development stage of the Wankel engine.

1.2 Continuous-combustion engines

The gas turbine has made tremendous progress in the last decade. It has the advantages of a higher power/weight ratio and less costly in large installation over the diesel engine. However, at present it cannot achieve the same fuel economy as the diesel engine, particularly at its part-load operating conditions. It is a strong competitor to the diesel engine and has established itself very firmly as a large standby, peak-load and emergency power unit, or as a constituent of a gas-turbine steam-turbine electricity generating power plant. In traction applications mainly at full-load operating conditions, the gas turbine shows an advantage for power plants over 300hp by offering less noise than its rivals, with reasonable fuel economy at full-load. With the latest combustion-chamber development based on premixed fuel systems and variable combustion-chamber geometry, it has no difficulty in satisfying the US pollution legislation. The use of new ceramic materials will permit the gas turbine to operate more efficiently at the higher

151

temperatures, indicating the further development potential of the automotive gas turbine. It is expected that in the next decade the gas turbine will compete successfully with the diesel engine in vehicle applications, particularly for the heavy truck.

Stirling and vapour engines give lower pollutant emission than all the other vehicle combustion engines. They also typify power plants with the lowest noise levels. When compared with the diesel engine they are more bulky, of lower power/weight ratio and more expensive to build. They also suffer from a major disadvantage for automotive use — an excessive starting-up time. At the present rate of development it seems that it is impossible to offer the Stirling engine as a large-scale alternative to the internal-combustion engine for automotive use within the next decade. The steam reciprocating engine is unlikely to be able to compete with the conventional internal-combustion engine on grounds either of cost or of fuel economy.

1.3 Electric vehicle engines

The electric power plant really offers hope as a satisfactory solution to pollution and noise in urban areas. Unfortunately a great deal of development and research is required before electrically powered cars can achieve techanical and economical acceptability to compete with the internal-combustion engine. Conventional storage batteries are unable to supply the specific power or specific energy of the i.c. engine. The development of new types of battery is essential. Fuel cells can provide good specific energy, but they have rather low specific outputs and are very expensive.

Although the electrically propelled car is not ready for the short-term period, its development should be encouraged because of its potential in the long term, particularly if the transport pattern of the future is to be based on central power stations.

The introduction of a hybrid combustion-electric engine looks very attractive from the pollution and fuel economy aspect and would greatly aid the development of the electrically powered car.

2 Long-term period

In the long-term, the lifetime of the internal-combustion engine will depend on the availability of natural liquid and gaseous fuel resources. The lifetime could also be extended if cheap synthetic fuels be developed from coal gasification or other sources. The gas turbine has a good chance of surviving in its closed-cycle form with external combustion or as an integral part of nuclear plant.

For long-term planning, however, the electrically powered vehicle seems to be the most favourable approach in meeting the environmental requirements.

An attempt to compare the different vehicle prime movers and their future potential has been made in the following Table. It shows the preference in numerical order.

Power plant	Suitable for		Noise level	Pollutant emission	Specific fuel consumption	Cost of engine relative to the spark-ignition engine
	Passenger car	Heavy truck				
Spark-ignition engine	1	3	3	3	3	1
Diesel engine	3	1	5	2	1	1·5
Rotary engine	2	3	3	4	4	1 to 1·5
Gas turbine	5	2	4	2	3	2 to 2·5
Stirling engine	6	4	1	1	2	3 to 5
Vapour engine	7	5	1	1	4	7
Storage battery	9	8	1	1	—	5
Fuel cell	8	7	1	1	2	10
Hybrid engine	4	6	2	1	2	5 to 10

Index

154